THE STORE OWNER'S GUIDE TO PRACTICAL RECORDKEEPING

THE STORE OWNER'S GUIDE TO PRACTICAL RECORDKEEPING

ROBERT C. RAGAN and M. ZAFAR IQBAL

CB

CONTEMPORARY
BOOKS

CHICAGO

Library of Congress Cataloging-in-Publication Data

Ragan, Robert C.
    The store owner's guide to practical recordkeeping / Robert C.
Ragan and M. Zafar Iqbal.
      p.   cm.
   ISBN 0-8092-3908-6 (paper)
   1. Bookkeeping.   2. Retail trade—Accounting.   I. Iqbal, M.
Zafar.   II. Title.
HF5635.R145   1992
657'.83902—dc20   91-40028
                                               CIP

Published by Contemporary Books, Inc.
180 North Michigan Avenue, Chicago, Illinois 60601
Manufactured in the United States of America
International Standard Book Number: 0-8092-3908-6

Contents

List of Exhibits

Preface

In *The Store Owner's Guide to Practical Recordkeeping*, the authors present a basic recordkeeping system primarily for the small-store owner-manager or prospective owner whose business does not justify hiring a trained, full-time bookkeeper.

This system will allow you to:

- maintain a record of all transactions of the business
- protect the assets of the business from errors, fraud, and carelessness
- provide a basis for business planning by showing the results of past decisions and furnishing the facts needed for future decisions

But this system will not allow you to attain these goals automatically. To be fully useful a bookkeeping system must be adapted to the needs of the individual business. Even then, it can only be as useful as it is up-to-date and accurate. The information it records must be applied not only to the preparation of tax returns but to the day-to-day operation of the business.

Introduction

If you own or manage a store, you can save hundreds, even thousands of dollars in bookkeeping fees by maintaining your own business records with this step-by-step guide to keeping the books for almost any type of retail or wholesale business.

From making the initial entry to closing the books, every aspect of bookkeeping is explained in detail here, including basic accounting reasoning and terms, recording accounts payables and receivables, reconciling a bank statement, handling payrolls, accounting for depreciable property, recording sales and returns, collecting and recording taxes, and more.

With illustrative, easy-to-follow examples and charts, *The Store Owner's Guide to Practical Recordkeeping* gives you, the small-business owner or manager the tools you need to effectively maintain your store's books, make the most of your assets, and increase your profitability.

PART I
THE WHY, WHAT, AND HOW OF RECORDS

1

1
Records—for the Government or for Yourself?

Why keep records?

If you are a typical small businessman or businesswoman, your answer to this question is probably, "Because the government [and you mean the Internal Revenue Service] requires me to!" If the question comes in the middle of a busy day, you may add a few heartfelt words about the amount of time you have to spend on records just for the government.

But is it "just for the government"? It shouldn't be. True, regulations issued in recent years, not only by the IRS but also by various other governmental agencies—federal, state, and local—have greatly increased the recordkeeping requirements of business. But the fact is that this may be a good thing for the small businessperson, overburdened though he or she usually is. Many studies have revealed a close relationship between inadequate records and business failures.

ADVANTAGES OF KEEPING GOOD RECORDS

A simple, well-organized system of records, regularly kept up, can actually save time by bringing order out of disorder. Furthermore, competition is very strong in today's business arena. A small businessperson needs to know almost on a day-to-day basis where the business stands regarding profit, which lines of merchandise or services are the most or the least profitable, what the working-capital needs are, and many other details. You can get this information with reasonable certainty only if you have a good recordkeeping system—one that gives you all the information you need *and no more.*

Good records can also help to safeguard your assets. Accurate records of cash transactions will disclose any shortages so that steps can be taken to find and correct the sources of trouble. Accounts-receivable records disclose any shortages in the customers' balances and also help to control bad-debt losses. Inventory shortages are somewhat harder to detect, but here again good records make it possible to keep the shrinkage to a minimum.

Still another important use of well-organized financial records is for the preparation of financial reports showing the progress and current condition of your business. Such reports can be invaluable if you need a bank loan or if the business must be evaluated for a sale or merger.

THE RECORDS ARE FOR YOU

Think of recordkeeping, then, not as a necessary nuisance imposed by governmental regulations but as an important tool for your own use in managing your business. Take the time, or hire an accountant, to set up a recordkeeping system that is patterned after basic accounting principles but is tailor-made for *your* store. Then grumble if you must, but *use it.* Remember, it is not just a storehouse of facts for government use; it is a source of information that can help you increase your profits if you put it to work constructively.

This book suggests a basic plan for building such a recordkeeping system.

2
Building Materials for Your Recordkeeping System

This chapter explains briefly some of the terms that are used over and over again in any discussion of financial records. If you are impatient, you can skip it and go directly to Chapter 3 and come back to this chapter if you have trouble later with some of the terms. However, you will find the rest of the book easier going if you do read this chapter and make sure before going on that you understand the basic ideas involved in financial record-keeping and the terms used.

ASSETS, LIABILITIES, AND CAPITAL

Anything a business *owns* that has a money value is an *asset* of the business. Cash, merchandise, supplies, amounts owed by customers (accounts receivable), land, buildings, furniture and fixtures, delivery equipment, and so on are assets.

Anything the business *owes* is a *liability*. Liabilities might include amounts owed to suppliers (accounts payable) or to the bank (notes payable), taxes already incurred but not yet due for payment, wages earned by employees since the last payday, and other amounts due.

The difference between what the business *owns* and what it *owes* is the amount that really belongs to the owner of the business—the owner's *equity* or *capital* (sometimes called *proprietorship*).

THE FRAMEWORK FOR YOUR RECORDS

Liabilities can be thought of as creditors' rights or claims against the assets of the business, and capital can be thought of as the owner's rights. The sum of these rights to the assets, of course, will always equal the sum of the assets themselves. In other words, the total assets always equal the total liabilities (creditors' rights) plus the capital (owner's rights), or simply:

$$\text{assets} = \text{liabilities} + \text{capital}$$

Let's see how two typical business transactions affect this equation. Suppose that you pay a bill from a supplier for $50. One of your assets, cash, will be reduced by $50. But a liability, accounts payable, will be reduced by the same amount, so the equation will still balance.

Now suppose you buy $50 worth of supplies and pay cash for them. Again the asset cash will be reduced by $50; but in this case the value of another asset, supplies, will be increased by $50. So the sum of all the assets doesn't change, and the equation still holds true.

This equation is known as the *accounting equation.* It is the framework on which you will build your financial records.

THE BASIC RECORDS

The financial records of a business begin with bits and pieces of paper: sales checks, credit memos, cash-register tapes, written receipts, check stubs, petty-cash slips, bank statements, and so on. These papers are important. They are the bricks from which you will build your organized, permanent records. Some sort of written record, however informal, should always be made *at the time a transaction takes place.*

The Journal: The information from these various papers is first brought together in one or more *journals*, sometimes called *books of original entry*. A journal is simply a record of the daily transactions of the business. Each journal entry shows (1) the date of transaction, (2) a brief description of it, (3) the amount of money involved, and (4) the assets, liabilities, capital, or type of income or expense affected by the transaction.

The Ledger: To make the information recorded in the journal more usable, each item is later transferred, or *posted*, to a ledger account. An *account* is a record of the increases and decreases in *one type* of asset, liability, capital, income, or expense. A book or file in which a number of accounts are kept together is called a *ledger*. Exhibit 11 in Chapter 14 shows typical accounts in a general ledger. A brief study of this will help you understand some of the following examples and transactions.

Sometimes the income and expense items are posted to a Profit-and-Loss Statement, and only the net profit or loss is posted to a ledger account. This method is used in the record-keeping system described in this book.

A business uses as many accounts as it needs for keeping track of its operations. A small firm with few pieces of equipment, for instance, may have only one account for all its equipment. A larger business will probably need an account for each type of equipment, or even in some cases for a single piece of equipment. A business with only one owner will need only one capital account; a partnership will need a capital account for each partner.

DOUBLE-ENTRY BOOKKEEPING

Notice that each of the transactions used to illustrate the accounting equation had two effects. This is true of all business transactions, since a transaction is basically an exchange of one thing for another. Double-entry bookkeeping shows this twofold effect by recording every transaction twice—as a *debit* entry in one account and as a *credit* entry in another. Either or both of the entries may be broken down into several items, but the total of the amounts entered as debits must equal the total of the amounts entered as credits.

DEBIT AND CREDIT ENTRIES

One account may have both debit (DR) and credit (CR) entries. Then what determines whether an entry is to be a debit or a credit? It depends on the type of account and on whether the transaction to be entered will increase or decrease the account. Exhibit 1 shows the types of entries (debit or credit) and the typical balances for each class of accounts.

Thus, as a study of Exhibit 1 will show, when you pay a bill, the amount paid is entered as a debit to accounts payable and as a credit to your cash account. When you buy supplies for cash, the amount paid is entered as a debit to the supplies account and as a credit to the cash account.

Each account sheet in the ledger has a column for the date, one for a brief description of the entry, one for the posting reference, and two for dollar amounts. Debit entries are always put in the left-hand dollar column, and credit entries in the right-hand column. If the debit entries in an account total more than the credit entries, the account is said to have a *debit balance*. If the credit entries total more than the debit entries, the account has a *credit balance*. The total of all the credit balances must equal the total of all the debit balances.

EXHIBIT 1: A TABLE OF DEBIT AND CREDIT ENTRIES

Type of account	If the transaction will *decrease* the account, enter it as a:	If the transaction will *increase* the account, enter it as a:	Typical balance
Asset	credit	debit	debit
Liability	debit	credit	credit
Capital	debit	credit	credit
Income	debit	credit	credit
Expense	credit	debit	debit

THE TRIAL BALANCE

To make certain that the sum of the debit balances does equal the sum of the credit balances, a *trial balance* is taken at the end of the month (or other accounting period). This is done simply by adding all debit account balances and all credit account balances. If no errors have been made, the two totals will be the same.

The trial balance ensures that any errors will be found before they are buried too deeply. It also clears the way for preparing financial statements.

FINANCIAL STATEMENTS

The journal alone would give you a complete record of all the transactions of your business, in simple chronological order. But that isn't enough. The ledger accounts are needed to organize the details from the journal into a usable form. You need to know where the business stands financially, how well it is doing, and what can be done to improve it. Ledger accounts provide for this information by grouping the transactions of your business in such a way that at any time you can prepare a Balance Sheet and a Profit-and-Loss Statement.

The *Balance Sheet* summarizes your assets, liabilities, and capital to show the condition of your business on a given date—what proportion of the assets you really own. It is called a Balance Sheet because it shows how the two sides of the accounting equation (assets = liabilities + capital) "balance" in your business.

The *Profit-and-Loss Statement* summarizes the activities of the business during the period covered. It shows the income and expenses of the business during that period and the profit or loss that resulted.

3
Methods and Equipment

The type of business you are in will affect the type of records you keep in a number of ways. Whatever system of bookkeeping you use, the details will have to be adapted to your special needs. It is important to have all the information you need for your own use in managing the business and for tax purposes. At the same time, your records should not be cluttered with details that aren't really necessary.

VARIATIONS IN METHODS OF KEEPING RECORDS

If a homemaker buys a bag of oranges for $2.50 from a small grocery store, a grocer using the simplest method of recordkeeping merely records the fact that a $2.50 sale has been made. He doesn't care whether the sale involves a bag of oranges or a pound of meat.

Another grocer might want to know that $2.50 worth of fresh produce, as opposed to meats or dry groceries, had been sold. Under normal circumstances, however, he wouldn't need to know whether the $2.50 entry on his financial records represented a bag of oranges or some other item of fresh produce.

But if, for instance, an appliance dealer sells a television set for $419.95, the dealer will want to record a number of facts in addition to the amount of the sale: the brand, the model number, trade-in information if applicable, the sales tax if any, the service contract charge if service is included, and so on.

Thus a grocer would not use the same bookkeeping system as an appliance dealer. In fact, in department or general-merchandise stores where both groceries and television sets are sold, different systems are generally used for recording sales in the different departments.

CASH AND ACCRUAL ACCOUNTING

Bookkeeping systems differ in the basic method of recording as well as in the amount of detail shown. For income-tax purposes, the IRS recognizes two basic methods: the *cash basis* and the *accrual basis.*

When books are kept on the cash basis, no income or expense is entered in the journal or ledger until cash is actually received or paid out. When the accrual basis is used, income from a sale or other income-producing transaction is entered as soon as the transaction takes place, even though the cash may not be collected until some future date. Likewise, in accrual accounting, expenses are recorded when they are incurred, even though payment may not be made until later.

Suppose, for example, that you sell $100 worth of goods on credit. If your books are kept on the accrual basis, the sale will be entered in the journal immediately. Later, when the account is paid, you will make another entry to record the payment.

If your books are kept on the cash basis, you will keep a memorandum record of each credit customer's account. A credit sale will be noted on this account but not entered in the journal until the bill is paid.

Now suppose you pay your employees every Friday, and December 31 falls on a Monday. If you use the accrual method, you will enter the amount of the wages earned between the end of the last pay period and the close of business on December 31 as a December expense, even though you pay it in January. If you keep your books on the cash basis, you will make no entry until you pay the employees on January 4.

WHICH METHOD IS BEST FOR YOU?

The IRS allows you to use either basis of accounting, cash or accrual, provided that (1) it clearly reflects income and (2) you use it consistently. IRS regulations state, however, that where inventories play an important part in accounting for income, the accrual method must be used in recording sales and purchases. Since this is the case in retail stores, *the bookkeeping system described in this book uses the accrual basis for purchases and sales. The cash basis is used for expenses and for income other than sales.*

THE RECORDS AND EQUIPMENT YOU NEED

The bookkeeping system described in the remaining chapters of this book is a modified double-entry system. It uses the following "books":

> *Sales and Cash Receipts Journal*
> *Cash Disbursements,*[1] *Purchases, and Expense Journal*
> *General Ledger* (a record of assets, liabilities, and capital)
> *Accounts Receivable Ledger*
> Employees' Compensation Record
> a business checkbook

These books, except for the checkbook, can be loose-leaf. Standard sheets can be purchased from an office-supply store. Many different types are sold, however. Study the bookkeeping system in relation to your own business before you make your choice.

------

[1] Payments you make to others, as distinguished from payments others make to you.

In addition to the books, several forms are needed. These are the following:

Daily Summary of Sales and Cash Receipts
Monthly customers' statements
Employees' pay slips
Petty-cash slips

Printed forms for all except the *Daily Summary* can be purchased at an office-supply store. The *Daily Summary* can be an inexpensive reproduction of a typewritten sheet on which you will fill in the figures.

Mechanical Equipment: In almost any type of business, an *adding machine* is needed, and if you have many transactions of the same or nearly the same type, a *cash register* is also desirable. The cash register might not be required if (1) you do not have too many transactions and (2) the transactions are varied enough so that a sales ticket or other record would have to be written out for most sales in addition to or instead of the cash-register "ring."

If a cash register is necessary for your business, care should be taken to select one that suits your needs. You will probably want a simple machine that prints on a tape the amount and one or two other details for each transaction and that gives you one or more totals at the end of the day. The most inexpensive machines give only one total of transactions, but various symbols can be produced on the register tape. These, with an adding machine, make possible a further breakdown of transactions. Usually a cash register that produces a receipt for the customer is desirable.

Small electronic calculators that multiply and divide are inexpensive, and you might find one of these quite useful. With a calculator you can quickly multiply and divide, compute discounts and sales taxes, figure payroll taxes, compute percentages, and make many other necessary calculations. Although these calculators also add and subtract, you should not use them in place of an adding machine to add long columns of figures, since they produce no tape that can be checked for errors.

Sales Checks: If you decide that you do not need a cash register, sales checks should be used to record all sales. Sales checks are a standard item carried by most suppliers of business forms. You may, however, want to have yours printed with the name, address, and telephone number of your store. The sales checks should be prenumbered. Use a system that makes it necessary to account for all sales-check numbers.

In some stores, sales checks are used for charge transactions even though cash sales are recorded on a cash register. Sales checks may also be written for cash "send" sales. A record of the charge sale is needed so that the customer's account can be debited; a record of the send sale is necessary so that delivery can be made to the proper address.

PART II
THE MONEY COMES IN— AND GOES OUT

4
The Change and Petty-Cash Fund

The recordkeeping system described in this book assumes that *all* receipts will be deposited in the bank. A combination change and petty-cash fund is used for all cash paid out other than by check. This practice makes it easier for you to account for cash receipts and gives you much better control over your cash.

THE CHANGE FUND

In any business where cash is received in over-the-counter transactions, it is necessary to make change. A *change fund* is kept on hand for this purpose.

The amount needed for making change varies with the size and type of business, and in some cases with the days of the week. Your daily balancing and recordkeeping will be easier, however, if you set a fixed amount for your change fund, large enough to meet all ordinary needs of the business. Then when the day's cash receipts are balanced and prepared for deposit, you will keep bills and coins totaling the fixed amount of the fund in the cash register for use the following day. Since you had this amount on hand before you made the day's first sale, the entire amount of the receipts for the day will still be available for deposit.

PETTY CASH

To avoid having to write many checks for small amounts, it is wise to have a *petty-cash fund* (a fixed amount) from which to make small payments. Each time a payment is made from this fund, a petty-cash slip similar to the one shown as Exhibit 2 should be made out. If an invoice or receipt is available, it should be attached to the petty-cash slip for filing.

The slips are kept with the petty cash. At all times, the total of the unspent petty cash and the petty-cash slips should equal the fixed amount of the petty-cash fund. When the total of the petty-cash slips approaches the fixed amount of the fund, a check is made out to "Petty cash" for the amount of the slips, and the money from this check is used to bring the cash in the fund back to the fixed amount.

EXHIBIT 2: THE PETTY-CASH SLIP

No. _____	Date _____
RECEIVED OF PETTY CASH	
Amount _____	
For _____	
Charge to _____	
Approved by:	Received by:
_____	_____

The petty-cash slips should be canceled or marked in such a way as to prevent their reuse. They are then summarized (that is, the slips are grouped according to the accounts to be charged, and the charges to each account totaled) and entered in the *Cash*

Disbursements Journal described in Part III of this book. A good way to handle these canceled slips is to summarize them on the outside of an envelope, showing also the date, check number, and amount of the check used to restore the petty-cash fund. The slips are then filed in the envelope.

A COMBINED CHANGE AND
PETTY-CASH FUND

In some cases, the petty-cash fund is kept in a box or safe, apart from the change fund. However, the same fund can serve for both petty cash and change. For example, if you decide that you need $50 for making change and $25 for petty cash, one $75 fund can be used. Whenever, in balancing the day's operations, you see that the petty-cash slips total more than $25, you can write a petty-cash check for the amount of the slips. The slips are then handled as explained in the preceding paragraph.

5
The *Daily Summary of Sales and Cash Receipts*

Whether you use a cash register or sales checks or both, all cash receipts and charge sales must be recorded. At the close of each day's business, the actual cash on hand is counted and balanced against the total of the receipts recorded for the day—that is, the sum represented by the total receipts must equal the cash on hand. This is done by means of the *Daily Summary of Sales and Cash Receipts* (Exhibit 3).

If you have more than one cash register, a *Daily Summary* should be prepared for each one. The individual summaries can then be combined into one overall summary for convenience in handling.

CASH RECEIPTS

The first section of the *Daily Summary*, "Cash Receipts," records all cash taken in during the day from whatever sources. This is the cash that must be accounted for over and above the amount that was in the change and petty-cash fund at the beginning of the day.

19

Cash Sales: The total of the cash sales is found simply by reading it from the cash-register tape or, if no cash register is used, by totaling the cash-sales checks.

Collections on Account: Whether or not collections on account are rung up on a cash register, you should keep an individual record of each customer making a payment. The amount to be entered on the *Daily Summary* is found by adding these receipts. If the collections are rung up on a cash register, the total is entered from the cash-register tape. The individual receipts should be added while the summary is being prepared, however, to make certain that their total agrees with the cash-register total. If the two totals do not agree, the error should be located immediately. This can be done by comparing the individual receipts with the collection-on-account items on the cash-register tape. Handling of such errors will be explained later in this chapter.

After any errors found have been corrected, the amount shown on the *Daily Summary* as "Collections on Account" should agree with the total of the customers' receipts. These receipts are then put aside and held for posting to the customers' accounts in the *Accounts Receivable Ledger*, as described in Part VII. Adding-machine tapes should also be kept for use if needed in checking customers' account balances.

Miscellaneous Receipts: Some cash receipts cannot be classified as cash sales or collections on account. They are entered on the *Daily Summary* as "Miscellaneous Receipts." These receipts might include refunds from suppliers for overpayments, advertising rebates or allowances, collections of rent from subleases or concessions, handling charges on coupons, and so on.

A sales check or other memo should be made out for each miscellaneous receipt of cash. These notations are totaled at the end of the day to give the amount entered as Item 3 of the *Daily Summary*. If you have a cash register with a key for miscellaneous receipts, the daily total of that register is used. The individual memos will still be necessary, however, because the miscellaneous receipts should be itemized on the back of the *Daily*

EXHIBIT 3: THE *DAILY SUMMARY OF SALES AND CASH RECEIPTS*

DAILY SUMMARY OF SALES AND CASH RECEIPTS

Date <u>MARCH 23, 19—</u>

CASH RECEIPTS

1. Cash Sales	$435.00
2. Collections on Account	100.00
3. Miscellaneous Receipts[1]	15.00
4. Total Receipts to Be Accounted For	$550.00

CASH ON HAND

5. Cash in Register:		
Coins	$ 25.00	
Bills	510.00	
Checks...............................	95.00	
Total Cash in Register		$630.00
6. Petty-Cash Slips		14.00
7. Total Cash Accounted For		$644.00
8. Less Change and Petty-Cash Fund:		
Petty-Cash Slips	$ 14.00	
Coins and Bills	86.00	
Change and Petty-Cash Fund [fixed amount]		100.00
9. Total Cash Deposit		$544.00
10. Cash Short (Item 4 less Item 9 if Item 4 is larger)		$6.00
11. Cash Over (Item 9 less Item 4 if Item 9 is larger)		—

TOTAL SALES

12. Cash Sales	$435.00
13. Charge Sales (sales checks #262 to #316)	225.00
14. Total Sales.....................................	$660.00

by <u>John Doe</u>

[1]Note to appear on back of summary: "Miscellaneous receipts: Refund on merchandise $15.00."

Summary. This information is needed for records that will be explained later.

Total Receipts: *After* the totals for the various types of cash receipts have been entered (Items 1, 2, and 3 of the *Daily Summary*), these totals are added to give Item 4, the total receipts for the day that must be accounted for.

HOW TO HANDLE ERRORS IN RECORDING COLLECTIONS ON ACCOUNT

Errors in recording collections on account may be of the following types:

- wrong amount rung up for the collection
- collection rung up on the wrong key (that is, as a cash sale or other transaction)
- collection not rung up
- no customer's receipt for a collection recorded on the cash-register tape

Errors of the first three types are easily identified and corrected on the cash-register tape and on the *Daily Summary.* Where there is no customer's receipt for a collection appearing on the cash-register tape, the error may be harder to find. A cash sale or other transaction may have been rung up as a collection on account; or the collection may have been rung up correctly but the receipt not prepared or prepared but lost or misplaced.

Sometimes the person who rang up the item will remember the transaction, and a correction can be made. If the collection cannot be identified, a dummy receipt should be made out showing the amount of the collection and marked "Unidentified receipt." Further handling of these unidentified receipts will be explained in the discussion of accounts receivable.

CASH ON HAND

The second section of the *Daily Summary*, "Cash on Hand," is a count of the cash actually on hand and the cash represented by petty-cash slips.

Cash in Register: The money in the cash register is counted at the close of business. Coins, bills, and checks are recorded separately and then totaled in Item 5 of the *Daily Summary*.

Petty-Cash Slips: Petty-cash slips represent cash that has been paid out. They are therefore totaled and included (Item 6) in the cash accounted for.

Total Cash Accounted For: After coins, bills, checks, and petty-cash slips have been entered, their total is recorded as Item 7. This total will include both the day's receipts and the amount that was on hand at the beginning of the day (the change and petty-cash fund).

Change and Petty-Cash Fund: Item 8 of the *Daily Summary* includes the petty-cash slips on hand (until they are replaced by cash as explained earlier) and enough cash to make up the fixed amount of the fund. The amount entered here for petty-cash slips is taken from Item 6. The amount of "Coins and Bills" is found by subtracting the total of the petty-cash slips from the fixed amount of the change and petty-cash fund.

Total Cash Deposit: The change and petty-cash fund is to be kept on hand for use in the next day's operations. Therefore, the amount to be deposited in the bank (Item 9) will be the total cash accounted for (Item 7) minus the fixed amount of the fund (Item 8). Since the fixed amount was in the change fund at the beginning of the day, the amount to be deposited should just equal the total receipts for the day (Item 4). If it does not, all work done in preparing the *Daily Summary* should be carefully checked, especially corrections to the cash-register tape. If no error is found in the counting and balancing, check the day's records for errors of the types listed in the box on page 24.

POSSIBLE ERRORS IN CASE OF
A CASH SHORTAGE OR OVERAGE

If the amount to be deposited is *more* than the total receipts recorded for the day, the overage could be caused by:

- neglecting to record or ring up a transaction
- recording or ringing up a transaction for too small an amount
- giving a customer too little change

If the amount to be deposited is *less* than the total receipts recorded for the day, the shortage could be caused by:

- recording or ringing up too large an amount for a transaction
- giving a customer too much change
- taking money from the cash register without recording it

Cash Short or Over: If the amount to be deposited and the total receipts for the day still do not agree after the day's work has been thoroughly checked, the difference is entered as "Cash Short" (Item 10) or "Cash Over" (Item 11). This completes the daily summary of cash receipts.

TOTAL SALES

The last section of the *Daily Summary of Sales and Cash Receipts* records the total sales for the day (Item 14) by adding the charge sales to the cash sales already entered as Item 1 of the summary. If you want a record of sales broken down by salespersons or departments, this can also be shown here.

The total of the charge sales is found by adding all the charge-sales checks. If charge sales are rung up on a cash register (which is usually not necessary), the total of the sales checks should be compared with the cash-register total as in the case of collections on account.

DEPOSITING THE RECEIPTS

As soon as possible after the *Daily Summary* has been completed, all cash for deposit should be taken to the bank. A duplicate deposit slip stamped by the bank should be kept with the *Daily Summary* as evidence that the deposit was made.

6
Writing the Checks

All major payments should be made by checks drawn on a bank account used only for business transactions. If your business is typical, you will have to write checks for merchandise purchases, employees' salaries, rent, utilities, petty cash, payroll taxes, and various other expenses.

YOUR CHECKBOOK

Your business checkbook should be the large desk-type checkbook. Such a checkbook usually has three checks to a page and large stubs on which to write a full description of each expenditure. It may have the name and address of your business printed on each check, and the checks should be prenumbered.

As each check is written, enter on the stub the date, payee, amount, and purpose of the payment. A running balance of the amount you have in the bank is maintained by subtracting the amount of each check from the existing balance shown on the check stub.

When a check is spoiled, tear off the signature part of the check to prevent any possibility of the check's being used, write

"VOID" prominently on the check and on the stub, and staple the torn check to the back of its stub. This assures you that the check will not be used in an unauthorized way.

SUPPORTING DOCUMENTS

Every check should have some sort of written document to support it—an invoice, petty-cash voucher, payroll summary, and so on. If such support is not available for some good reason, a memo should be written stating what the check is for.

Each of these supporting documents should be approved, by signature or initials, by you or someone you have authorized to do so. The signature should indicate that the goods or services have been received, that the terms and price are correct, and that no error has been made in computing the amount to be paid. It is especially important to see that offered cash discounts are correctly computed and deducted.

When each check is written, the supporting document should be marked "Paid" and the date and check number shown. If the checks are prepared for your signature by an employee, you should see the supporting document before you sign the check. Make certain that it is marked in a way to prevent its being paid a second time. After payment has been made, this supporting material should be filed in a paid-bills file in alphabetical order by payee.

PAYING THE BILLS

Bills are usually paid once a month unless there are special discount terms or special arrangements with suppliers for daily or weekly settlement. Most vendors send monthly statements, often in addition to delivery tickets and/or invoices for each individual purchase. Before the monthly statement is paid, the items on it should be checked against the individual invoices for correctness and to make sure that no item on the statement has already been paid on the basis of its invoice. Any balance brought forward from an earlier month should also be carefully checked to make sure that it is correct and has not already been paid.

RECONCILING YOUR BANK STATEMENT

The bank will periodically send you your canceled checks and a statement of your bank account. Some banks send out statements once a month on various days of the month. Others, particularly in the case of accounts without much activity, send out statements less often. However, you can arrange with your bank to have your statement sent each month as of the last business day of the month. This will make it easier for you to *reconcile* your records with the bank statement—that is, to compare the two records and account for any differences.

Reconciling your bank statement every month without fail is an important step in keeping accurate records. Even if someone else does the rest of your recordkeeping, you should do the bank reconciliation yourself. How this is done is explained in detail in Part IV.

PART III
LINING UP THE RECORDS

7
The *Sales and Cash Receipts Journal*

The *Daily Summary of Sales and Cash Receipts* is in effect a worksheet for figuring and recording the results of a single day's business. The *Sales and Cash Receipts Journal* brings together on one page the information from a number of *Daily Summary* forms. This provides a better permanent record and makes the information easier to work with for various purposes. Some entries on a typical page from a *Sales and Cash Receipts Journal* are shown as Exhibit 4.

ENTRIES FROM THE *DAILY SUMMARY*

Usually total sales, charge sales, collections on account, and the total cash deposit can all be entered on the same line of the journal. The date should be entered, "Daily summary" written in the description column, and the money amounts entered from the summary to the corresponding journal columns. Note that each column is marked (DR) or (CR) to indicate whether the entries in that column are normally debit or credit entries. If it is necessary to make a debit entry in a credit column or a credit entry in a debit column, that entry is enclosed in parentheses or written in red. When the columns are totaled, these entries will be subtracted instead of added.

Illustration I on Exhibit 4 shows the entries that would be made in the *Sales and Cash Receipts Journal* from the *Daily Summary of Sales and Cash Receipts* shown in Exhibit 3. The amounts entered under "Total Sales," "Collections on Account," and "Total Cash Deposit" are taken from the *Daily Summary* items having the same identification as the journal columns. The amount entered under "Charges to Customers" is from Item 13, "Charge Sales," of the *Daily Summary*.

If you have provided separate lines on the *Daily Summary* for receipts from sources other than sales or collections on account, you should have corresponding columns in the *Sales and Cash Receipts Journal*. These columns should follow the "Collections on Account" column, and they will be credit columns.

As each day's entries are made in the journal, the amount entered in the "Total Cash Deposit" column is also entered as a deposit in your checkbook and added to the previous balance.

MISCELLANEOUS RECEIPTS

Items included in "Miscellaneous Receipts" on the *Daily Summary* and itemized on the back of the summary sheet must be identified in the description column of the *Sales and Cash Receipts Journal*. They will therefore need separate lines. The amounts are entered under "General Ledger Items" or under "Miscellaneous Income and Expense Items."

Miscellaneous receipts that represent either refunds on expense items or income not due to sales are entered in the credit column under "Miscellaneous Income and Expense Items." These include receipts from such sources as rent collections, interest, refunds from suppliers, and advertising rebates. Cash over and cash short are also entered here: cash over as a credit and cash short as a debit.

Miscellaneous receipts that do not represent income or expense items are entered in the credit column under "General Ledger Items." These might include such receipts as additional

EXHIBIT 4: THE SALES AND CASH RECEIPTS JOURNAL

Date 19—	Description and/or Account	PR	Total Sales (CR)	Charges to Customers (DR)	Collections on Account (CR)	Miscellaneous Income and Expense Items (DR)	(CR)	General Ledger Items (DR)	(CR)	Total Cash Deposit (DR)
Illustration I: Entries from Exhibit 3										
Mar 23	Daily summary		660 00	225 00	100 00					544 00
	Refund on merchandise						15 00			
	Cash short					6 00				
	Exchange									
Illustration II: Entries from Exhibit 16										
Mar 23	Daily summary		660 00	225 00	100 00					562 00
	Refund on merchandise						15 00			
	Cash short					6 00				
	Exchange								18 00	

investment in the business or a loan from your bank. In most small businesses, the "General Ledger" column of the *Sales and Cash Receipts Journal* is seldom used.

ENTRIES FROM OTHER SOURCES

Cash receipts are sometimes entered in the journal from sources other than the *Daily Summary*. For example, if your bank grants you a loan, they will probably just credit the amount of the loan to your bank account and send you a notice that this has been done. Since no cash is actually received as part of the day's operations, the money need not be included in your *Daily Summary*. It can be entered directly in the journal. The description will be "Notes payable—bank loan," and the amount will be entered under "Total Cash Deposit" and in the credit column under "Ceneral Ledger Items."

Another example is a transaction that you do not want to appear in the *Daily Summary* because you wish to keep it confidential—for instance, the investment of additional capital in the business. A separate deposit can be prepared and entered in the journal.

CHECKING YOUR ENTRIES

After the day's entries in the *Sales and Cash Receipts Journal* have been made, the work should be checked by adding all entries in the debit columns and all entries in the credit columns. The two totals should be the same.

Since the *Daily Summary* has already been checked, any errors here are simply mistakes in transferring the figures from the summary to the journal. They can easily be found and corrected.

FILING THE RECORDS

When these steps have been completed, charge-sales tickets and records of collections on account are put aside to be recorded in the individual customer accounts, as explained in Part VII. The

Daily Summary, cash-register tapes, cash-sales tickets, adding-machine tapes, and any other written records used in the balancing are filed by date.

PREPARING THE MONTHLY TOTALS

At the end of the month, each column in the journal is totaled, and the totals are checked in the way described for daily entries. The "Miscellaneous Income and Expense" entries and the "General Ledger" entries are summarized so as to give a single figure for each account or type of expense appearing in the columns. Cash overages and shortages are combined to give the net cash overage or shortage for the month.

It is a good idea to enter the column totals lightly in pencil until you have reconciled your bank statement as explained in Part IV. After you have made any adjustments or corrections made necessary by the reconciliation, the column totals should be entered in ink.

8
The *Cash Disbursements, Purchases, and Expense Journal*

If possible, the checks drawn should be entered daily in the *Cash Disbursements, Purchases, and Expense Journal* (Exhibit 5). Be careful to see that *every* check number is accounted for in the journal. If a check is spoiled, write "VOID" in the payee column, enter the check number, and leave all other columns blank. Some typical entries are shown in Illustration I of Exhibit 5. (Entries shown in Illustrations II and III of Exhibit 5 are described in subsequent parts of this book.)

The *Cash Disbursements, Purchases, and Expense Journal* shown in Exhibit 5 has a minimum number of columns. It is quite possible, for instance, that you will need more than two columns for payroll deductions. Also, if some types of expense normally require several payments a month (for instance, operating supplies, delivery expenses, postage), additional columns should be provided for them. Expenses that normally have only one or two payments a month (such as rent, telephone, electricity, and so on) are entered in the debit column under "Miscellaneous Income and Expense Items," with the account shown for each.

The "General Ledger" columns of the *Cash Disbursements Journal* are used only for entries that directly affect the assets,

EXHIBIT 5: THE CASH DISBURSEMENTS, PURCHASES, AND EXPENSE JOURNAL

Date 19—	Payee and/or Account	Ch. No.	Amount of Check (CR)	Merchandise Purchases (DR)	Gross Salaries (DR)	Payroll Deductions Income Tax (CR)	Payroll Deductions Soc. Sec. (CR)	Miscellaneous Income and Expense Items (DR)	Miscellaneous Income and Expense Items (CR)	General Ledger Items (DR)	General Ledger Items (CR)
Jul 1	John Smith—rent	92	200 00					200 00			
14	ABC Company	93	115 00	115 00							
19	Z Company—furn. and fix.	94	30 00							30 00	
	VOID	95									
20	Payroll	96	50 85		58 50	5 90	1 75				

Illustration I: Miscellaneous entries—rent, merchandise purchase, asset purchase, spoiled check, payroll

Illustration II: Accounts payable   A—Accounts payable recorded

Jul	31	Accounts payable		275 00			300 00
		Furniture and fixtures			25 00		

B—Accounts payable reversed

Aug	1	Accounts payable		(275 00)		300 00	
		Furniture and fixtures					25 00

C—Accounts payable paid

Aug	5	Z Company—furn. and fix.	101	25 00		25 00
	7	ABC Company	102	175 00	175 00	
	12	XY Corporation	103	100 00	100 00	

Illustration III: Check to restore change fund when checks cashed for customers total more than receipts to be deposited

Aug	18	Exchange	111	18 00	18 00

liabilities, and capital of the business, as recorded in the *General Ledger* (explained in Part VI). Some examples are purchases of furniture or equipment, payment of bank loans, and drawings of the proprietor or partners.

Some checks may include disbursements that are chargeable to more than one account—petty-cash checks, for instance. In such a case, the amount chargeable to each account (for example, postage, small purchases of supplies, minor repairs) is recorded on the supporting document and on the check stub and entered in the proper column of the journal. If this results in more than one entry in the same column, a separate line is used for each entry. The next check is then entered on the next unused line.

PAYROLL ENTRIES

You will note that columns are shown for gross salaries and for federal income-tax and Social Security deductions. In some areas, a state or local payroll tax may also have to be withheld. Or you may have other payroll deductions, such as for group hospitalization or savings bonds. A column should be provided for each type of deduction.

In some localities and types of businesses, salaries are paid in cash rather than by check. In such cases, one check should be drawn to "Payroll" for the total net pay and cashed at the bank. The cash is then distributed to the employees in pay envelopes showing gross pay, deductions, and net pay. A signed receipt should be required from each employee. The entries in the *Cash Disbursements Journal*, taken from a payroll summary, are the same as when payment is made by check except that only one check number will be shown. Payroll records and payroll taxes are discussed further in Part X.

OWNERS' WITHDRAWALS

If your business is an individual proprietorship or a partnership and you or other partners withdraw fixed amounts regularly as "salaries," these withdrawals are not treated as employees' salaries. They should *not* be entered in the "Gross Salaries" column. They are not subject as salaries to federal withholding or Social Security taxes, although they could be subject to other payroll deductions. They are described as *proprietor's drawings* and entered either in the "General Ledger" debit column or in a separate column if their frequency justifies it. If there are partners, a separate drawing account is maintained for each.

When payroll deductions are made from the proprietor's drawings, enter (1) the amount of the check, (2) the deductions, and (3) proprietor's drawings equal to the amount of the check plus the deductions.

If your business is a corporation, you are an employee, and any salary paid you is treated just like that paid other employees.

Merchandise Withdrawn by the Owner: If your business handles consumer goods, you and your family are probably among its "customers." You may be tempted to take the items you need out of stock without making any record of them. But you should not do this, any more than you should take cash from your cash register without a record.

There are several reasons for this. For one thing, withdrawing merchandise without recording it has the effect of reducing the profits of your business, and hence your income taxes. In effect it gives you a tax deduction for personal living expenses. Naturally the IRS takes a dim view of such a procedure. It is one of the matters the IRS particularly looks into when examining the income-tax returns of a small business. Not recording merchandise taken from stock also distorts the operating results of the business and increases inventory shortages.

On the other hand, withdrawals of merchandise for your personal use should not be treated as ordinary sales. To do this would result in including "profits" on these withdrawals in income of the business and would increase your income tax unnecessarily. To prevent this, merchandise withdrawn for your own use should be recorded at cost rather than at selling price. Also, it is best to treat it as a deduction from purchases rather than as a sale at cost value, since the latter would tend to distort your gross margin.

If the withdrawals are only occasional, they can be entered individually in the *Cash Disbursements, Purchases, and Expense Journal* by a deduction (in parentheses) in the "Merchandise Purchases" column and a debit entry in the "General Ledger" column, with the account designated as "Drawing account" or "Proprietor's drawings." If withdrawals are frequent, a tally can be kept throughout the month, and only one entry made in the journal at the end of the month.

For a discussion of how to arrive at the cost, see "Merchandise Inventories" in Part IV. If a tally is kept of all withdrawals during the month, it may be easier to keep this by selling price and reduce the total to cost at the end of the month by the gross-margin method explained in Part IV.

MONTH'S-END PROCEDURES

At the end of the month, each column of the *Cash Disbursements, Purchases, and Expense Journal* is totaled. Items appearing in the "Miscellaneous Income and Expense" and "General Ledger" columns should be summarized so that only one total is shown for each account.

You can check your column totals by adding all debit-column totals and all credit-column totals. The two totals should be the same.

Column totals should be entered lightly in pencil until their accuracy has been further proved by your bank-account reconciliation. After any necessary adjustments or corrections have been made, the final totals should be entered in ink.

Three further steps are needed before you are ready to prepare the monthly financial statements: reconciling your bank account, setting up your accounts payable, and counting or estimating your merchandise inventory. These steps will be discussed next.

PART IV
GETTING SET FOR
MONTHLY FINANCIAL
STATEMENTS

9
Reconciling Your Bank Statement

Before starting to check, or *reconcile*, your bank statement, you should check your own figures. Your *General Ledger* (explained in Part VI) will include an account "Cash in Bank." Beginning with the bank balance shown in this account at the end of the preceding month, add the total cash deposited during the month, and subtract the total cash disbursements. (These figures are the penciled totals from the "Total Cash Deposit" column of the *Sales and Cash Receipts Journal* and the "Amount of Check" column of the *Cash Disbursements, Purchases, and Expense Journal.*)

The result should agree with your checkbook balance at the end of the month. If it does not, an error has been made in entering or adding one or more items in either the checkbook or the journals. Such errors can be found by taking the following steps:

1. Add check amounts recorded on check stubs to make sure that the total agrees with the "Amount of Check" column of the *Cash Disbursements Journal.* If it does not, check the individual amounts.

2. Add the deposit amounts recorded on the check stubs to make sure that the total agrees with the "Total Cash Deposit" column of the *Cash Receipts Journal.* If it does not, check the individual amounts.

3. Recompute the running balance in your checkbook to make sure that the additions and subtractions are correct.

RECONCILING YOUR RECORD WITH THE BANK'S

When you are sure that the balance in your checkbook is mathematically correct, you are ready to reconcile your record with the bank's. You will need the preceding month's reconciliation, the checkbook stubs, and the canceled checks and bank statement received from the bank. Then take these steps:

1. Arrange all the canceled checks in numerical order.

2. Compare deposits listed on the bank statement with deposits entered in your checkbook. List in the first section of the reconciliation (Exhibit 6) any deposits recorded in your checkbook during the month but not appearing on the bank statement. (If deposits are made daily, only one or two deposits at the end of the month should have to be put on this list.)

3. There will probably be some canceled checks from the previous month. Check these off on the list of outstanding checks shown on the preceding month's reconciliation. List in the first section of the current reconciliation the checks still outstanding.

4. Check off on the corresponding check stubs all canceled checks drawn during the month being reconciled. Add the checks recorded on the remaining stubs to the list of outstanding checks on the reconciliation. (Disregard any checks that you may have written after the end of the month.)

EXHIBIT 6: A BANK RECONCILIATION

BANK RECONCILIATION NOVEMBER 30, 19—

Balance per bank statement		$793.94
Add deposits not credited:		
November 29	$247.52	
November 30	302.19	549.71
		$1,343.65
Deduct outstanding checks:		
No. 913—10/20	$30.18	
929—11/15	10.14	
935—11/25	142.60	
939—11/30	82.60	
940—11/30	95.80	
941—11/30	74.50	435.82
Adjusted balance per bank statement		$907.83
Balance per checkbook		$903.58
Add:		
Check No. 920 entered as $58.30 should be $53.80	$4.50	
Deposits of Nov. 1 recorded as $298.60 should be $299.60	1.00	5.50
		$909.08
Deduct bank service charge		1.25
Adjusted balance per checkbook		$907.83

---

5. If any errors in amounts are discovered in the preceding steps, list them in the second section of the reconciliation statement and adjustments to be added or deducted.

6. Examine the bank statement for service charges or other adjustments to your account and enter them in the second section of the reconciliation.

7. Carry out the additions and subtractions shown on the bank reconciliation. The adjusted balance per bank statement should equal the adjusted balance per your checkbook.

Errors Made by the Bank: Occasionally you may find that the bank has made a mistake in your account. The following types of errors can occur:

- Deposit or check of another person posted to your account
- Your deposit or check posted to another person's account
- Deposit or check posted in the wrong amount
- Preceding month's balance incorrectly brought forward on your bank statement
- Addition or subtraction incorrectly carried out on the bank statement

Any such errors should be reported to the bank at once. They must also be shown as adjustment items in the first section of your bank reconciliation. When the next month's bank statement is received, make sure that any bank errors from the previous month have been corrected in the statement.

RECORDING ADJUSTMENTS

Any adjustments to your own records made in reconciling your bank statement must be entered in your checkbook and also in the journals as follows:

If a check was recorded in the wrong amount:

- Enter the amount of the adjustment in the "Amount of Check" column of the *Cash Disbursements Journal* with an explanation.
- Enter the same amount in the other column in which the check was originally entered.
- If the check was recorded as less than the correct amount, simply enter the adjustment in the two columns. This will have the effect of an addition. If the check was recorded as more than the correct amount, enter the adjustment as a deduction (in parentheses or in red).
- If the second entry is in the "Miscellaneous Income and Expense" column or the "General Ledger" column, the

adjustment will be entered there as a debit if the check was recorded as less than the correct amount and as a credit if it was recorded as more than the correct amount.

If a deposit was recorded in the wrong amount:

■ Enter the amount of the adjustment in the "Total Cash Deposit" column of the *Cash Receipts Journal.*

■ If the adjustment can be identified with a specific receipt, it should also be entered in the column for that type of receipt. It is more likely, however, that the error was made in balancing the day's work. In that case, it should be entered as a shortage or overage.

■ If too small an amount was recorded for the deposit, the adjustment should be entered in the journal as an addition; if too large an amount, as a deduction. If the second entry is in the "Miscellaneous Income and Expense" or "General Ledger" column, the adjustment will be entered there as a credit if the amount recorded for the deposit was too small and as a debit if the amount recorded was too large.

   Bank service charges are entered in the "Amount of Check" column of the *Cash Disbursements Journal* and as a debit in the "Miscellaneous Income and Expense Items" column. Your checkbook balance should be corrected by adding or subtracting the net adjustment.

THE FINAL CHECK

When all adjustments have been recorded and the corrected totals of the two journals inked in and posted to the *General Ledger*, the balance of the "Cash in Bank" account of the ledger should agree with the adjusted balance shown on the bank reconciliation.

10
Recording Accounts Payable

Since inventories are an important factor in accounting for the income of a store, IRS regulations require that you record merchandise purchases and sales on an accrual basis. This means that you must set up accounts payable for all purchases that have not been paid for. For income-tax purposes, you only need to record accounts payable at the end of the year. For your own purposes, it is best to set them up at the end of each month in order to keep your monthly statements from being distorted.

SETTING UP ACCOUNTS PAYABLE

You should have an unpaid-bills file into which all delivery tickets or invoices for charge purchases are put. If you do not receive an invoice or delivery ticket, make a memo of the purchase, and put it in the file. All unpaid statements from vendors should also be kept in this file.

When a bill is paid, all delivery tickets, invoices, and statements having to do with it are taken from the file and kept as supporting documents of the payment. Thus at any time, the items in the unpaid file represent all purchases that have not been paid for.

At the end of the month, a list of the unpaid items is drawn up showing vendors and amounts. The amounts are then added to give the total accounts payable for that month. If any items are represented only by delivery tickets or memos with no price given, an estimate of the price should be made and used in listing the accounts payable.

RECORDING ACCOUNTS PAYABLE IN THE *CASH DISBURSEMENTS JOURNAL*

The total of the accounts payable is entered in the *Cash Disbursements, Purchases, and Expense Journal.* If only merchandise purchases are involved, enter the total in the "Merchandise Purchases" column and in the "General Ledger" credit column, with the account shown as "Accounts payable." If other items are involved, they will be entered in the columns to which they apply (usually as a debit in the "General Ledger" or "Miscellaneous Income and Expense" column), with the account shown. In either case, the total of the accounts payable is entered as a credit in the "General Ledger" column. (See entry A dated July 31, in Illustration II of Exhibit 5.)

The effect of these entries is to include all purchases in the month in which they were made, whether or not they have been paid for. The entries may be made either before or after the bank reconciliation, since cash is not affected.

REVERSING THE ENTRIES

If nothing further were done about them, the entries described above would require special handling of checks written during the next month to pay any of the accounts included in the total. This can be avoided by *reversing* the accounts-payable entries. Under this method, the first entry in the *Cash Disbursements, Purchases, and Expense Journal* each month is the reverse, or opposite, of the accounts-payable entry made in the preceding month. This means that the amounts entered in the preceding month as additions will now be entered in the same columns as deductions; those entered as debits will now be entered as credits. The accounts-payable total entered in the "General Ledger" column as a credit is now entered in that column as a debit. (Note how the August 1 entry B in Exhibit 5 "reverses" the July 31 entry.)

RECORDING PAYMENTS OF THE ACCOUNTS

When checks are drawn to pay for purchases included in the preceding month's accounts payable, they are entered like any other check. Each of these purchases will thus have been added twice (once as an account payable and once as a disbursement) and deducted once (as a reversing entry). This has the effect of leaving the purchase as a charge in the month in which the purchase was made, even though the check is drawn and recorded in the following month. Study the entries in Illustration II of Exhibit 5.

11
Merchandise Inventories

One of the most important steps in the preparation of financial statements is the obtaining of accurate inventory figures. There are a number of methods of keeping *perpetual* or *book inventories*, but a really accurate inventory can be obtained only by counting all the merchandise on hand: a *physical inventory*. If a book inventory has been kept also, a comparison of the two inventories may reveal inventory shortages or overages.

Many small merchants, however, do not want to take on the clerical work of maintaining perpetual inventory records. At the same time, they do not feel that a physical inventory every month is justified. In such cases, the inventory can be estimated for monthly statements and a physical inventory taken only at the end of the year.

ESTIMATING THE INVENTORY

Inventory can be estimated by the gross-margin method. Under this method, you assume that the gross margin (sales less cost of goods sold) for the period is going to be a certain percentage of your sales. The gross-margin percentage for the period between the last two physical inventories is most often used for this. The cost of sales for the current period will then be the cost-of-sales percentage (100 percent less the gross-margin percentage) times the sales for the period. Ending inventory is then computed as in the following example.

Suppose that your sales for the month are $10,000, that your inventory at the beginning of the month was $3,000, and that your merchandise purchases during the month amount to $6,000. You estimate your gross margin at 25 percent of sales. Your ending inventory can be computed as follows:

Beginning inventory....................	$3,000	
Merchandise purchases................	6,000	
Merchandise available for sale		$9,000
Estimated gross-margin percentage	25	
Cost-of-sales percentage (100 − 25)	75	
Sales for the month	$10,000	
Cost of goods sold (75 percent of $10,000)		7,500
Ending inventory.....................................		$1,500

If you use the gross-margin method of computing your inventory, it should be applied separately to each department. This method can give fairly accurate results for monthly financial statements under some circumstances, but the fact remains that it produces only an estimated inventory. As often as practicable, you should make a physical count rather than an estimate.

An alternative to a complete physical inventory every month is counting some departments each month and using the gross-margin method for other departments. The departments are scheduled so that each one is counted every two or three months.

COUNTING THE MERCHANDISE

How often should you take a physical inventory, actually counting the items on your shelves? That depends on the type of business you are in and whether you have a reliable book-inventory system. In all cases, a physical inventory should be taken at least once a year, usually as of the close of your fiscal year. If accurate book inventories cannot be maintained, a monthly physical inventory may be needed for financial statements. In some businesses or departments where turnover is rapid, a weekly physical inventory is helpful, although usually such an inventory would not be converted to dollars.

Preparations for Taking Inventory: To ensure accuracy in counting, care should be taken to see that merchandise is in good order in the bins, compartments, or on the shelves. It is often impractical to try to take an accurate inventory during business hours, so the actual counting must usually be done in the evening or over a weekend. However, the orderly arranging of merchandise, instructions to the counters, and perhaps the counting of reserve stock should be done ahead of time.

A part of your planning for taking inventory should be to establish shipping and receiving "cutoffs"—that is, to make certain (1) that all items entered in your books as purchased before the inventory have been received and are counted, and (2) that all items recorded as sold before the inventory are removed and not counted.

If the type of merchandise you are counting requires weighing or any other kind of measuring, the equipment that will be needed for this should be on hand.

The Tally Sheets: In some types of business, a complete description of each item by brand, container size, and so on is needed. In these cases, inventory tally sheets showing this information should be prepared in advance so that the only writing necessary is to record the quantities counted. These sheets should have space for inserting the unit prices and extending the dollar value of the stock. The order of the items on the list should follow as closely as possible the order in which the stock is arranged in the store. Separate sheets should be prepared for separate departments.

If you think you do not need tally sheets, you can take

inventory on *tags*. A tag is placed with each different item in stock before the count. The description of the item and the number of units in stock are then entered on the tag by the counters. Here too it is advisable to have space on the tag for the price and extension.

If a great many tags or tallies are used, they should be numbered. This is necessary to make sure that none are lost or misplaced after the count is made and before the final summarizing of the inventory valuation. Tag or tally numbers can also be used to identify the department involved.

In some cases, a complete description of the items is not necessary; the number of items and the price might be enough for the counters to enter. The department should always be identified, however, by marking or physical separation of the tags or tallies.

Counting by Teams: It may be helpful to have one person count and call to another person who does the writing. Sometimes, to ensure accuracy a second person or team counts the items again. If this is done, the tag or tally may be left with the merchandise after the first count, to be removed after the final count. To get a completely independent check, a duplicate sheet or tag stub can be used for the second count. The two counts should then be compared, and any discrepancies corrected by a third count.

If you have a number of people taking part in your inventory, you may want to have the names or initials of persons counting, listing, or checking entered on each tag or tally.

PRICING THE INVENTORY

After the physical counting of your inventory has been finished, each item must be priced. A generally accepted method of pricing inventories is valuation of the items at cost or market value, whichever is lower.

Cost is the price for which you purchased the item. Theoretically this would be the invoice price plus freight-in, less any discounts taken. In a small retail business, however, the factor of freight-in will generally not be material and can probably be ignored. Discounts will probably not be significant, either. If a small cash discount is applicable to most of your purchases, you could make a percentage reduction in the overall inventory rather than try to reduce the price of the individual items.

Market value would be one of the following:

1. the replacement price of the item
2. if the item has been marked down, your current asking price less your normal gross margin
3. scrap or salvage value if the item is no longer salable at retail

The Retail Method of Valuing Inventory: You can avoid computing the cost of each item by using the *retail method* of valuing your inventory. Under this method, retail prices of the items are entered on the tally sheet or tag as the count is made. The retail value of the inventory for each department is then totaled and reduced by the year-to-date gross-margin percentage for the department.

In the case of marked-down items, the marked-down retail price should be used. (All appropriate markdowns should be made before taking the inventory.) If any unsalable merchandise is on hand, it should not be included in this computation but should be valued at scrap or salvage value if any.

Some types of merchandise, such as meats and fresh produce, fluctuate so widely in price that the retail method of pricing cannot be used. Fortunately there are usually not too many different items on hand in these departments. Pricing them at your current cost is not difficult.

Coded Costs: Another method for determining cost prices for inventory valuation is to have the merchandise marked with a coded cost as well as a retail price at the time it is put on sale. A letter code can be devised by using a ten-letter key word with no letter repeated, for example:

1 2 3 4 5 6 7 8 9 0
P U R C H A S I N G

Thus an article that cost $3.17 and sells for $5.00 would be marked "RPS $5.00." In taking inventory, the counters enter the decoded cost price on the tag or tally.

The practice of marking merchandise with a coded cost is common in gift shops, jewelry stores, and other stores where turnover is comparatively slow and items have a rather high gross-margin and unit value. It serves primarily as a guide to management in making markdowns and sometimes in bargaining with customers. Its use in inventory valuation is limited by (1) the work involved in coding the merchandise in the first place and (2) the fact that decoding of prices by the inventory takers can be troublesome and subject to errors. Also, the work must be reviewed to make certain that no cost prices are higher than market.

Total Dollar Valuation: After all inventory items have been priced, the total dollar values are found by multiplying the prices by the quantities. This is usually done on the tag or tally sheets containing the quantities counted. The amounts on the tags or tally sheets for each department are then added to give the total for the department. *Accuracy is important.* It is advisable to have the work checked for clerical and arithmetical errors.

PERPETUAL INVENTORY RECORDS

Some merchants keep a *continuous,* or *perpetual,* book record of their inventory. A detailed explanation of this method is beyond the scope of this book; it is described here only briefly. If you want to use it, you should have a qualified accountant set up the system for you and explain its use in detail.

PART V
THE SCORE—WIN OR LOSE, AND HOW MUCH?

12
The Profit-and-Loss Statement

As soon as possible after the end of the month, you should have completed the following procedures, or as many of them as apply to your business. (Chapter numbers refer to the chapter in this book in which the procedures are explained.)

1. entered all cash transactions in the *Sales and Cash Receipts Journal* (Chapter 7) and the *Cash Disbursements, Purchases, and Expense Journal* (Chapter 8)
2. reconciled your bank account (Chapter 9)
3. established the amount of your accounts payable and entered it in the *Cash Disbursements, Purchases, and Expense Journal* (Chapter 10)
4. billed your customers and balanced your accounts receivable (Chapter 16)
5. established the amount of your ending inventory (Chapter 11)
6. made any necessary noncash entries, such as allowance for bad debts (Chapter 18) and depreciation
7. totaled and balanced your journals (Chapters 8 and 9)

If you keep your records by departments, you should also have posted your Departmental Purchases and Sales Record and prepared your Statement of Departmental Operations. (These records will be discussed in the next chapter.)

You are now ready to prepare your monthly financial statements—the *Profit-and-Loss Statement* and the *Balance Sheet*—and to post your *General Ledger*. (The Balance Sheet and the *General Ledger* are discussed in Part VI.)

Exhibit 7 shows a typical Profit-and-Loss Statement for a single proprietorship or a partnership. This statement shows the results of operations for the month and for the year to date, with percentages based on net sales. The list of expenses is only a suggestion. You can add or delete items according to the requirements of your business.

WHERE THE FIGURES COME FROM

Amounts in the "This Month" column of Exhibit 7 are determined as follows:

- Line 1, "Net Sales." Enter the total of the column headed "Total Sales" in the *Sales and Cash Receipts Journal* less any debits to sales from the summary of the "Miscellaneous Income and Expense Items" column in the *Cash Disbursements Journal.*
- Line 2, "Beginning Inventory." Enter the ending inventory of the previous month from the "Merchandise Inventories" account in the *General Ledger.*
- Line 3, "Merchandise Purchases." Enter the month's total from the "Merchandise Purchases" column of the *Cash Disbursements Journal* less any credits to purchases from the summary of the "Miscellaneous Income and Expense Items" column in the *Cash Receipts Journal.*
- Line 4, "Merchandise Available for Sale." Add purchases to beginning inventory (line 2 plus line 3).
- Line 5, "Less Ending Inventory." Enter the total ending inventory found by using one of the methods explained in Part IV.

EXHIBIT 7: THE PROFIT-AND-LOSS STATEMENT

STATEMENT OF PROFIT AND LOSS
XYZ STORE

MONTH OF _____ 19___ AND _____ MONTHS ENDED _____, 19___

	This Month		Year to Date	
	Amount	Percent of sales	Amount	Percent of sales
1. Net Sales	$ _____	100	$ _____	100
Less Cost of Goods Sold:				
2. Beginning Inventory	_____		_____	
3. Merchandise Purchases	_____		_____	
4. Merchandise Available for Sale ..	_____		_____	
5. Less Ending Inventory	$ _____		$ _____	
6. Cost of Goods Sold	$ _____		$ _____	
7. Gross Margin	$ _____	_____	_____	_____
Less Expenses:				
8. Salaries and Wages	_____		_____	
9. Rent	_____		_____	
10. Utilities	_____		_____	
11. Repairs and Maintenance	_____		_____	
12. Delivery Expense	_____		_____	
13. Supplies	_____		_____	
14. Advertising	_____		_____	
15. Depreciation	_____		_____	
16. Bad Debts	_____		_____	
17. Taxes and Licenses	_____		_____	
18. Insurance..................	_____		_____	
19. Interest	_____		_____	
20. Other Expenses.............	$ _____		$ _____	
21. Total Expenses	$ _____	_____	$ _____	_____
22. Operating Profit (Loss)	_____		_____	
23. Other Income	_____		_____	
24. Net Profit (Loss)	$ _____	_____	$ _____	_____

60

- Line 6, "Cost of Goods Sold." Enter merchandise available for sale less ending inventory (line 4 less line 5).
- Line 7, "Gross Margin." Enter net sales less cost of goods sold (line 1 less line 6).
- Line 8, "Salaries and Wages." Enter the total of the "Gross Salaries" column in the *Cash Disbursements Journal.*
- Lines 9 through 20, "Expenses." Enter amounts from the summary of the "Miscellaneous Income and Expense Items" column in the *Cash Disbursements Journal* (debits) less any credits to the same expenses from the corresponding column in the *Cash Receipts Journal.* (You may have provided separate columns in the *Cash Disbursements Journal* for some recurring expenses. If so, enter the totals of these columns less any credits on the proper lines.)
- Line 21, "Total Expenses." Enter the total of the expenses recorded on lines 8 through 20.
- Line 22, "Operating Profit (Loss)." Enter gross margin less total expenses (line 7 less line 21); if the business suffers a loss, line 21 less line 7.
- Line 23, "Other Income." Enter any income items not already taken care of from the summary of the "Miscellaneous Income and Expense Items" column in the *Cash Receipts Journal* (such as interest income or other income not directly related to the operations of the business) less any debits to the same categories from the corresponding column in the *Cash Disbursements Journal.*

You may have provided separate columns in the *Sales and Cash Receipts Journal* for recurring items of other income. If you want your Profit-and-Loss Statement also to show some types of "other income" separately, more than one line can be used.

- Line 24, "Net Profit (Loss)." Operating profit plus other income (line 22 plus line 23).
- If your business is a corporation, line 24 will read, "Net Profit Before Income Taxes," and two lines will be added:

- Line 25, "Income Taxes." Enter from the "Miscellaneous Income and Expense Items" column of the *Cash Disbursements Journal.*
- Line 26, "Net Profit." Net profit before income taxes less income taxes (line 24 less line 25).

POSTING REFERENCES

As each amount is entered from its journal to a line on the Profit-and-Loss Statement, a check mark (✓) should be made beside the amount in the journal. After all lines on the Profit-and-Loss Statement have been entered, the journals should be reviewed to make sure that the totals of the following columns have check marks:

✓ The "Total Sales" column in the *Cash Receipts Journal*
✓ The "Merchandise Purchases" and "Gross Salaries" columns in the *Cash Disbursements Journal*
✓ The summaries of the "Miscellaneous Income and Expense" columns in both journals
✓ Any additional columns you have provided for other income or expense items

THE YEAR TO DATE

Before going on with the Profit-and-Loss Statement, you should post your *General Ledger* as described in Part VI. The balancing of the ledger will prove the accuracy of all your entries up to this point, and you will then be ready to go on to the "Year to Date" and percentage columns on your Profit-and-Loss Statement.

For the first month of the year, the figures for the year to date will be identical to those for the month. For all other months, each year-to-date figure will equal the current month's figure plus the year-to-date figure from the preceding month's statement.

Exceptions to this are figures having to do with beginning and ending inventories. Beginning inventory in the "Year to

Date" column remains the same throughout the year. It is always the beginning inventory established at the beginning of the year. Merchandise available for sale in the "Year to Date" column is always beginning inventory plus the year-to-date merchandise purchases. Ending inventory in the "Year to Date" column is the same as that in the "This Month" column.

THE PERCENTAGES

The percentages are obtained by dividing each amount by the net sales for the period. Percentages are not usually computed for lines 2 through 5. Percentages can then be computed only for lines 6, 8 through 20, and 23 (and for corporations, line 25). The percentages for the remaining items can be found by adding or subtracting. Then each net-profit percentage should be checked by dividing the net-profit dollar figure by the corresponding net sales figure.

It should be noted that percentages in the "Year to Date" column must be computed. They cannot be found by adding the month's percentages to the year-to-date percentages from the preceding month, as was done with the dollar amounts.

13
Departmental Operating Records

If you sell several different types of merchandise, you will find it helpful to organize your operations and your recordkeeping by departments. The primary purpose of this is to get a better picture of your operating results. Even though your overall operations may be profitable, you may find by keeping departmental records that one department is producing most of the profits while others are barely breaking even or perhaps even losing money. You can then attack the problem of what to do to improve the profits of the departments with a poor showing. You may even decide to drop a department or reduce its activities.

There are other advantages to keeping records by department. Many statistics about typical operations are available through trade associations, governmental publications, and so on. These statistics can be very useful in finding weak spots in your own store's performance. But they are published on a departmental basis. Unless your business is largely a one-department operation, they would be useless for comparison with figures covering your whole store.

Gross-margin percentages from departmental records can

be used to estimate inventories by the gross-margin method (Part IV), where an overall percentage could be misleading. Also, items subject to a sales or excise tax can be segregated from items not subject to such taxes.

How far you want to departmentalize will depend on the size and nature of the business. A grocery store, for example, might have some or all of the following departments: fresh produce, meats, bakery products, dairy products, frozen foods, dry groceries, and taxable items (if you are in a jurisdiction where foods are not taxed). A drugstore, with the many products carried today, might have any number of departments. Don't overdo it, though. A specific type of merchandise or service should not be set up as a separate department unless the volume of sales justifies such a separation.

DEPARTMENTAL PURCHASES
AND SALES RECORD

The basic tool for breaking down your records by departments is a *Departmental Purchases and Sales Record* (Exhibit 8). The departments are identified here by numbers to give the illustration more general application, but you will probably find it more satisfactory to name the departments. Also, if you have many departments, one page may be used for purchases and another page for sales.

Entering Departmental Purchases: The amount entered in the "Total Purchases" column of the Departmental Purchases and Sales Record should, of course, equal the sum of the amounts entered for the individual departments. It should also agree with the merchandise purchases for that day shown in the *Cash Disbursements Journal.*

The breakdown by departments is obtained by analyzing the invoices paid or set up as accounts payable. Each invoice should be marked to show to which department it is charged. In some cases, one invoice may be distributed to more than one department. In that case, the amount charged to each department should be shown on the invoice.

EXHIBIT 8: THE DEPARTMENTAL PURCHASES
AND SALES RECORD

		Purchases			Sales		
Date	Explanation	Total	Dept. 1	Dept. 2	Total	Dept. 1	Dept. 2

Entering Departmental Sales: The breakdown of sales by departments is obtained from the *Daily Summary of Sales and Cash Receipts* if shown there, or by analysis of sales checks and cash-register tapes. The amount entered in the "Total Sales" column should equal the sum of the entries for the individual departments and should agree with the total sales for that day shown in the *Sales and Cash Receipts Journal.*

Other Entries: Occasionally an entry in the Departmental Purchases and Sales Record may be necessary to record transactions other than purchases or sales. For example, a refund from a vendor might be received and recorded in the *Sales and Cash Receipts Journal* as a reduction in purchases, or a check might be drawn to a customer as a refund and recorded in the *Cash Disbursements Journal* as a reduction in sales. Since these entries are not routine, they should be entered on a separate line in the Departmental Purchases and Sales Record with an explanation.

Monthly Totals: At the end of the month, the columns should be added and the totals checked horizontally. That is, the total of the month's purchases for the individual departments should equal the sum of the "Total Sales" column. Also, the total purchases should agree with the month's total of the "Merchandise Purchases" column in the *Cash Disbursements, Purchases, and Expense Journal* less any items entered as return sales or refunds in the *Cash Disbursements Journal.*

STATEMENT OF DEPARTMENTAL OPERATIONS

A *Statement of Departmental Operations* should be prepared at the end of each month. This statement shows totals for the month and for the year to date (see Exhibit 9). The sales and purchases for the month are entered directly from the Departmental Purchases and Sales Record. The sales and purchases for the year to date are computed by adding this month's figures to the year-to-date amounts from the previous month's statement.

The beginning inventory for the month is the same as the ending inventory on the previous month's statement. The beginning inventory for the year to date is the inventory as of the beginning of the year and will be the same throughout the year. The ending inventory will be the same for the month and for the year to date. It can be found by one of the methods described in Part IV.

The gross-margin amount as computed for the year to date should equal the month's gross margin plus the year-to-date gross margin from the previous month's statement. The gross-margin percentage for the month will usually not be exactly the same as the gross-margin percentage for the year to date, but if the two percentages differ very much, all figures and computations should be checked for accuracy. It is possible, however, that such variations might be due to seasonal clearances, markdowns, and so on.

Direct Departmental Expenses: The Statement of Departmental Operations may end with the gross-margin percentages. However, if you have expenses that can be assigned to specific departments, you can if you wish continue the statement and reduce the gross margin by these direct departmental expenses. This will show the contribution each department makes to overhead expenses and profits.

If this is done, care should be taken to assign expenses fairly. Where a direct expense can easily be assigned to one department, that department should not be penalized just because a corresponding expense cannot be assigned so easily to another department. For example, a butcher's entire salary could probably be assigned to the meat department of a grocery store, while one or more sales clerks serve all the other departments. It would not be right to charge the meat department with the butcher's salary unless the sales clerks' salaries are allocated to the other departments.

The departmental contribution may be more useful than the gross margin of the department. However, you should not complicate your recordkeeping by trying to allocate overhead expenses that are difficult if not impossible to assign accurately.

Using the Percentages: Exhibit 9 shows percentages as well as dollars for both gross margins and departmental contributions. The percentages are valuable for comparing your departmental figures with those of other stores or with your own figures for other periods. When you compare the departments of your store with one another, however, percentages can be misleading, because the gross-margin percentages on some types of items are typically lower than on others.

Often a more rapid turnover and other factors make up for a low gross-margin percentage. For example, in a small grocery store, the gross margin might be about 16 percent of sales; in a small retail jewelry store, nearly 50 percent of sales. But in the grocery store, inventory would typically turn over about once a month; in the jewelry store, only about once a year. Expenses in the grocery store would typically be about 11 percent of sales, leaving a 5 percent net profit; in the jewelry store, expenses would typically be about 46 percent of sales, leaving a net profit of 4 percent. Thus, if you had both a jewelry and a grocery department in your store, it would be unrealistic to compare the gross-margin percentages of the two departments.

Departmental Turnover: The departmental turnover, which shows how fast your merchandise is moving, is another useful

EXHIBIT 9: THE STATEMENT OF DEPARTMENTAL OPERATIONS

STATEMENT OF DEPARTMENTAL OPERATIONS

YOUR STORE

MONTH OF _____ 19___ AND _____ MONTHS ENDED _____, 19___

	Total		Department 1		Department 2	
	This Month	Year to Date	This Month	Year to Date	This Month	Year to Date
Net Sales	$____	$____	$____	$____	$____	$____
Less Cost of Goods Sold:						
Inventory at Beginning of Period	____	____	____	____	____	____
Merchandise Purchases	____	____	____	____	____	____
Merchandise Available for Sale	____	____	____	____	____	____
[Beginning inventory plus merchandise purchases]						
Less Inventory at End of Period	____	____	____	____	____	____
Cost of Goods Sold	$____	$____	$____	$____	$____	$____
[Merchandise available for sale less ending inventory]						
Gross Margin	$____	$____	$____	$____	$____	$____
[Sales less cost of goods sold]						
Gross Margin Percentage	____	____	____	____	____	____
[Gross margin divided by sales]						
[The following is optional]						
Direct Departmental Expenses:						
Salaries and Wages	____	____	____	____	____	____
Rent	____	____	____	____	____	____
Depreciation of Special Equipment	____	____	____	____	____	____
Other	____	____	____	____	____	____
Total Direct Departmental Expenses	$____	$____	$____	$____	$____	$____
Departmental Contribution	$____	$____	$____	$____	$____	$____
[Gross margin less direct departmental expenses]						
Departmental Contribution Percent	____	____	____	____	____	____
[Departmental contribution divided by sales]						
Turnover Per Month	____	____	____	____	____	____
[Cost of goods sold divided by average inventory. In "Year to Date" column, divide this result by the number of months included. Average inventory is beginning inventory plus ending inventory, divided by two]						

measure for comparing the performance of a department with similar departments in other stores or the performance of one period with another. It should be noted that the turnover figures in Exhibit 9 show monthly turnover. Most published turnover figures are annual. To convert the monthly figures to annual figures, multiply them by twelve.

PART VI
THE SHAPE YOU'RE IN

14
The *General Ledger* and the Balance Sheet

After the income and expense accounts from your journals have been posted to the Profit-and-Loss Statement, you will find that a number of totals in the journals are still unchecked. Most of these will be posted to asset and liability accounts in the *General Ledger*.

An example of a standard *General Ledger* sheet is shown as Exhibit 10. A sheet should be provided for each asset, liability, and capital account. Often each account is given a number for convenience, but this is optional. Exhibit 11 shows a typical chart of accounts for the *General Ledger* of a small store. You may not need all the accounts shown—land and buildings, for instance, if you rent your place of business. On the other hand, you may want to add some accounts.

POSTING FROM THE
SALES AND CASH RECEIPTS JOURNAL

The "Total Sales" column and the summary of the "Miscellaneous Income and Expense Items" column in the *Cash Receipts Journal* have already been posted to the Profit-and-Loss Statement. The remaining column totals are posted to the *General Ledger* as follows:

- The "Charges to Customers" column is posted in the debit column of the "Accounts Receivable" account.
- The "Collections on Account" total is posted in the credit column of the "Accounts Receivable" account.
- The "General Ledger" columns have already been summarized by accounts. Each net total, debit or credit, is posted in the proper column of the corresponding account in the *General Ledger*.
- The "Total Cash Deposit" column is posted in the debit column of the "Cash in Bank" account.

POSTING FROM THE
CASH DISBURSEMENTS JOURNAL

The columns headed "Merchandise Purchases," "Gross Salaries," and "Miscellaneous Income and Expense Items" in the *Cash Disbursements Journal* have already been posted to the Profit-and-Loss Statement. The other column totals are posted to the *General Ledger* as follows:

- The "Amount of Check" column is entered in the credit column of the "Cash in Bank" account.
- Payroll deductions are entered in the credit columns of the corresponding accounts.
- The general ledger items have already been summarized by accounts, as in the *Cash Receipts Journal*. Each net total, debit or credit, is posted to the corresponding *General Ledger* account.

FINISHING TOUCHES IN THE
JOURNALS AND LEDGER

As in posting to the Profit-and-Loss Statement, when each total is posted from the journals, a check mark should be made beside the column total in the journal to show that it has been posted.

Entries in the *General Ledger* should be dated as of the end of the month to which they apply. The posting reference in the *General Ledger* (column headed "PR" or "Ref.") should be "CR" for the *Cash Receipts Journal* or "CD" for the *Cash Disbursements Journal*, followed by the number of the journal page from which the item was posted.

As each entry is made in the ledger, the balances should be brought up to date. Entries should be made in ink except for the "Balance" column. This may be kept in pencil for ease of correc-

EXHIBIT 10: A *GENERAL LEDGER* SHEET

ACCOUNT:					NO.		
			Items posted		**Balance**		
Date	Description	PR	Debit	Credit	Debit	Credit	

tion in case an error is made in addition or subtraction. The balance should at all times equal the difference between the total of all postings to the debit column and the total of all postings to the credit column. It will appear in whichever column has the larger total.

OTHER POSTINGS

You may have provided a separate column in your *Cash Receipts Journal* for sales taxes (which will be discussed in Part X). The total of this column should be entered in the credit column of the "Sales Tax Payable" account of the *General Ledger*. When the tax is paid, a debit entry from the *Cash Disbursements Journal* will offset the credit entry from the *Cash Receipts Journal.*

If you use an "Exchange" account as described in Part VIII, the credits recorded in the *Cash Receipts Journal* should just equal the debits recorded in the *Cash Disbursements Journal.* The account should therefore always have a zero balance and may if you wish be omitted from the *General Ledger.* The "Exchange" totals in the journals would then be marked with an "X" instead of a check mark to show that they are not posted.

If you are a member of a credit plan, you probably have a separate column in your *Cash Receipts Journal* for discounts on credit-plan sales. The total of this column is entered on your Profit-and-Loss Statement as an expense. It should also be posted in the *General Ledger* as a credit to accounts receivable. Two check marks should be made beside the column total to show that it has been posted twice.

RECORDING ENDING INVENTORY

After all postings to the *General Ledger* have been made from the journals, an entry must be made in the "Merchandise Inventories" account to record your ending inventory. There should already be a debit balance in the account equal to the beginning inventory shown on line 2 of the "This Month" column of your Profit-and-Loss Statement. An entry is now made to increase or decrease this amount to the ending inventory shown on line 5 of

EXHIBIT 11: A CHART OF *GENERAL LEDGER* ACCOUNTS

ASSETS

[All asset accounts except those marked "CR." normally have debit balances.]

Current Assets
100   Cash in Bank
105   Petty Cash
110   Exchange account
120   Accounts Receivable
125   Allowance for Bad Debts *(CR.)*
130   Merchandise Inventories

Fixed Assets
150   Land
160   Buildings
165   Allowance for Depreciation—Buildings *(CR.)*
170   Delivery Equipment
175   Allowance for Depreciation—Delivery Equipment *(CR.)*
180   Furniture and Fixtures
185   Allowance for Depreciation—Furniture and Fixtures *(CR.)*
190   Leasehold Improvements
195   Allowance for Amortization—Leasehold Improvements *(CR.)*

LIABILITIES[1]

[All liability accounts normally have credit balances.]

Current Liabilities
200   Accounts Payable
205   Notes Payable—Current
210   Income Taxes Withheld—Federal
215   Income Taxes Withheld—State
220   Social Security Tax Payable
225   Sales Tax Payable

Long-Term Liabilities
250   Notes Payable—Long-Term

CAPITAL²

[All capital accounts except those marked "DR." normally have credit balances.]

300 Proprietor's Capital
310 Proprietor's Drawings *[DR.]*
350 Profit and Loss *(CR. if profit; DR. if loss)*

¹If the business is a corporation, the liability accounts will also include the following:
230 Federal Income Tax Payable
235 State Income Tax Payable
²The capital accounts listed here are for a single proprietorship. If the business is a partnership, capital and drawing accounts are provided for each partner. If the business is incorporated, the capital accounts are as follows:
300 Capital Stock
310 Retained Earnings
320 Dividends Paid *(DR.)*
350 Profit and Loss *(CR. if profit; DR. if loss)*

---

the Profit-and-Loss Statement. The amount of the entry is the difference between the beginning and ending inventories. If the ending inventory is larger than the beginning inventory, the entry will be a debit; if the ending inventory is smaller than the beginning inventory, the entry will be a credit.

For example, if your beginning inventory as shown in the *General Ledger* and the Profit-and-Loss Statement is $6,000 and the ending inventory $7,500, you will make a debit entry of $1,500 in the "Merchandise Inventories" account of the *General Ledger*. Since the balance of the "Inventories" account is always a debit balance, this entry will raise the balance to $7,500, the ending inventory figure.

If with the same beginning inventory your ending inventory is $5,000, you will make a credit entry of $1,000. This will reduce the $6,000 balance to $5,000.

The posting reference for this entry is "INV."

BALANCING THE LEDGER

You are now ready to balance the *General Ledger* by adding all the debit balances and all the credit balances. The difference between these two totals should equal the net profit or loss for the month shown on your Profit-and-Loss Statement. If the debits total more than the credits, your business has made a profit; if the credits total more than the debits, it has suffered a loss.

If the profit or loss shown by the totals of the *General Ledger* balances equals that shown on your Profit-and-Loss Statement, this amount is posted to the "Profit and Loss" account in your *General Ledger*, as a credit if it represents a profit and as a debit if it represents a loss. The debits and credits in the ledger should now balance.

But what if, when you compare the difference between the debit and credit balances in the *General Ledger* with the month's profit or loss as shown by the Profit-and-Loss Statement, the two figures do not agree? There are only a few areas where an error could have been made. Follow the steps listed in the box in this chapter to identify the mistake before you post the profit or loss to the *General Ledger*.

PREPARING THE MONTHLY BALANCE SHEET

A *Balance Sheet* is a summary of the *General Ledger* accounts. In contrast to the Profit-and-Loss Statement, which covers an entire accounting period, the Balance Sheet is for a specific date. Therefore, it does not have this-month or year-to-date figures. It is usually desirable, however, to show the balances as of the same date in the current year and in the preceding year.

An example of a Balance Sheet for a single proprietorship is shown as Exhibit 12. It simply lists the accounts as they appear in the *General Ledger* with their balances and with the additions and subtractions necessary to show the total assets, liabilities, and capital. (This example shows only the current year.) Remember that "the balance sheet must balance"—that is, total assets must equal total liabilities plus capital.

HOW TO IDENTIFY ERRORS IN
COMPUTING PROFIT OR LOSS

If the difference between the debit and credit balances in the *General Ledger* does not agree with the profit or loss shown on the Profit-and-Loss Statement, take the following steps to find your mistake:

- Find the amount of the difference. Is it just twice the amount of some journal posting or *General Ledger* balance? If so, that posting or balance was probably treated as a debit instead of a credit, or as a credit instead of a debit.
- Check the additions of the Profit-and-Loss Statement and of the *General Ledger* balances.
- Check both journals to see that all items that should have been posted to either the Profit-and-Loss Statement or the *General Ledger* were correctly posted.
- Check each journal to see that the total of all debit items posted equals the total of all credit items posted.
- Check to see that the beginning-of-the-month and end-of-the-month balances of the "Merchandise Inventories" account in the *General Ledger* agree with the same items on the Profit-and-Loss Statement.
- Check the *General Ledger* to see (1) that the debit balances equaled the credit balances before this month's postings and (2) that the balance in the "Profit and Loss" account agrees with the year-to-date profit or loss figure in the preceding month's Profit-and-Loss Statement.

EXHIBIT 12: THE BALANCE SHEET

ABC STORE

BALANCE SHEET, _____, 19____

ASSETS

Current Assets:
Cash:
    Cash in Bank .... $_____
    Petty Cash .... _____ $_____
Accounts Receivable .... $_____
Less Allowance for Doubtful
    Accounts..................... _____
Merchandise Inventories .... _____
Total Current Assets............ $_____
Fixed Assets.
    Land.......................... $_____
    Buildings .... _____
    Delivery Equipment .... _____
    Furniture and Fixtures .... _____ $_____
      Less Allowance for
      Depreciation............... _____
       $_____
Leasehold Improvements, Less
    Amortization .... _____
    Total Fixed Assets .... _____
Total Assets .... $_____

LIABILITIES AND CAPITAL[1]

Current Liabilities:
Accounts Payable.............. $_____
Notes Payable, Due Within One
    Year .... _____
Payroll Taxes and Withheld
    Taxes .... _____
Sales Taxes .... _____
    Total Current Liabilities .... $_____
Long-Term Liabilities:
Notes Payable, Due After One
    Year .... _____
Total Liabilities .... $_____
Capital:
Proprietor's Capital, Beginning
    of Period .... $_____
Net Profit for the Period ...... $_____
Less Proprietor's Drawings[2] ... _____
Increase in Capital .... _____
    Capital, End of Period ...... _____
Total Liabilities and Capital .... $_____

[1]For partnership or corporation, see footnotes to Exhibit 11.
[2]If the business suffers a loss, the proprietor's drawings will be *added* to
the net loss to give the total *decrease* in capital.

15
Steps to Be Taken
at the End of the Year

Most businesses maintain accounting and tax records on an annual basis. In many cases, a calendar year ending December 31 is used, but it may be a fiscal year ending with the last day of any month. There may be advantages in adopting a fiscal year other than the calendar year if (1) your business is seasonal and inventories and accounts receivable are lower at a time of the year other than December 31, or (2) the demands of your business in the spring make it hard for you to find time to prepare a tax return.

CLEARING AWAY THE DEADWOOD

Whether your accounting is done on a fiscal-year or calendar-year basis, steps must be taken at the end of the year to *close your books*.

1. Bring your depreciation schedules up to date as described in Part IX. Normally your depreciation entry in the *Cash Disbursements Journal* for the last month of the year will

bring your books into agreement with your depreciation schedules.

2. Review your accounts receivable with the thought of charging off all bad debts and any long-standing differences between your detailed records and the *General Ledger* account. Also, review your allowance for bad debts, and make any adjustments needed. (See Part VII.)

3. Review your inventory valuation to make sure that no unsalable or slow-moving merchandise is being carried at too high a value.

4. Review your bank reconciliation, and consider writing off any checks that have been outstanding for a long time (at least a year). To write off a check, make an entry in the *Cash Disbursements Journal* reversing the entry made when the check was drawn. The amount of the check is entered as a deduction (in parentheses or in red) in the "Amount of Check" column and as a credit under "Miscellaneous Income and Expense Items," with the account listed as "Other income." The amount is also added to the balance in your checkbook.

These steps should be taken *before you prepare your financial statements for the last month of your accounting year*. The year-to-date profit or loss shown on the final statements will be the figure you use for tax-return purposes.

If your business is a corporation, the final tax liability should also be computed so that it can be included in your statements. If you cannot compute the exact tax liability before closing your books, the closest possible estimate should be made. Any minor difference between the estimated tax recorded for the year and the final tax paid can be added to or deducted from the next year's income tax on your statements. A large difference, however, should appear on your next year's Profit-and-Loss Statement as "Overestimate (Underestimate) of Last Year's Taxes."

CLOSING THE "PROFIT AND LOSS" AND "PROPRIETOR'S DRAWINGS" ACCOUNTS

After the steps listed above have been completed, the "Profit and Loss" account and the "Proprietor's Drawings" account in the *General Ledger* are *closed into* the "Proprietor's Capital" account. No entries are needed in the journals.

For a sole proprietorship, the closing entries in the *General Ledger* are as follows:

1. If you have a profit, the amount of the profit is entered as a debit in the "Profit and Loss" account and as a credit in the "Proprietor's Capital" account.
2. If you have a loss, the "Profit and Loss" account is credited and the "Proprietor's Capital" account debited for the amount of the loss.
3. The total of the "Proprietor's Drawings" account is then credited to that account and debited to the "Proprietor's Capital" account.

These entries reduce the "Profit and Loss" and "Proprietor's Drawings" accounts to zero.

If your business is a partnership, each partner's drawings account is closed into his or her capital account, and the profit or loss distributed to the capital accounts. Just how this is done depends on the partnership agreement.

If your business is a corporation, the "Profit and Loss" account is closed into the "Retained Earnings" account. The "Dividends Paid" account is closed by crediting that account and debiting the "Retained Earnings" account for the amount of the dividends paid. This entry reduces the "Dividends Paid" account to zero.

THE FINAL BALANCE

After these closing entries have been made, your *General Ledger* should still be in balance: that is, the sum of the credit balances

should equal the sum of the debit balances. Some business owners prefer to start a new year by bringing forward, or transferring to new ledger sheets, all the *General Ledger* account balances, but this is not necessary. If it is done, the new ledger
sheets should be checked to make certain that the total of the
debit balances still equals the total of the credit balances. This
will show up any errors that may have been made in copying the
balances onto the new sheets.

PART VII
THE ABSENTEE ASSET:
ACCOUNTS RECEIVABLE

16
Recording Accounts Receivable

If you extend credit to your customers, you must keep an accurate account of the amount each customer owes you and be systematic about billing and collections. This is important. It results in better relations with your credit customers and in fewer losses from bad debts.

THE *ACCOUNTS RECEIVABLE LEDGER*

The simplest method of handling accounts receivable (other than just keeping a file of sales-slip carbons) is to have a ledger sheet, or account, for each credit customer. These accounts are kept in an *Accounts Receivable Ledger* in alphabetical order. After the *Daily Summary of Sales and Cash Receipts* has been completed, the charge-sales checks and cash-receipts slips for payments on account are arranged in alphabetical order and posted to the individual customers' accounts in the ledger.

Exhibit 13 shows a typical *Accounts Receivable Ledger* sheet. For each credit sale, the entry should show the date, the sales-check number, and the amount of the sale, which is recorded in the debit column. Returned sales are also recorded in the debit column, but as a deduction (that is, in red or in parentheses). Collections on the account are entered in the credit column. After each entry, the new balance should be computed by adding sales to the previous balance or deducting cash receipts and returns.

THE ACCOUNTS RECEIVABLE CONTROL SHEET

In addition to the individual customer accounts, a control sheet should be set up. The same form is used for the control sheet as for the individual accounts. The total charges to customers and total collections on account are entered on this sheet from the *Daily Summary*, charges in the debit column and collections in the credit column. A running balance is maintained as for the individual customers' accounts. (See Exhibit 14.)

At any time, the balance on the control sheet should equal the total of the balances of all the individual accounts. If it does not, follow the procedure outlined in the box later in this chapter. When you first set up your records and whenever you assign your recordkeeping to a new person, it is best to check the balances after each day's posting. Later, as the daily balancing and posting become routine, the check may be made weekly; and then if no problems occur, only at the end of the month.

This check shows whether your accounts are mathematically correct, but it does not show whether any postings have been made to the wrong customer's account. This problem and the resulting harm to your customer relations can only be avoided through care on the part of the person keeping your records or by having the work reviewed by another person.

If you are able to balance your accounts receivable each month without difficulty, you can do away with the accounts-receivable control sheet and balance your accounts directly to the *General Ledger* "Accounts Receivable" account. In any case, the balance on the control sheet of the *Accounts Receivable Ledger* should agree with the balance of the *General Ledger*

EXHIBIT 13: THE *ACCOUNTS RECEIVABLE LEDGER:*
CUSTOMER'S ACCOUNT

JOHN DOE
345 SIXTH STREET

Date		Item	Debit		Credit		Balance	
Sep	1	Balance					47	62
	8	Sales check #195	4	50			52	12
	10	Received on account			47	62	4	50
	19	Sales check #231	42	50			47	00
	20	Sales check #243, return sale	(35	00)			12	00

"Accounts Receivable" account at the end of each month.

When the day's posting has been finished, the sales checks and cash-receipts tickets should be filed by dates.

BILLING CUSTOMERS

At the end of each month, a statement should be sent to each of your customers whose account has a balance. You may have your statement forms printed so as to show the name, address, and telephone number of your business. However, standard statement forms can be bought, and you can write, type, or stamp the information on them.

Each customer's statement is essentially a copy of his or her ledger sheet for that month. The beginning balance, sales, re-

EXHIBIT 14: THE *ACCOUNTS RECEIVABLE LEDGER:* CONTROL SHEET

ACCOUNTS RECEIVABLE CONTROL SHEET								
Date		Item	Debit		Credit		Balance	
Nov	1	Balance brought forward					2395	00
	1		80	00			2475	00
	2		230	00	195	00	2510	00

turns, cash payments, and ending balance are shown. A photocopy of the statement should be made for your records.

A Time-Saver: If your business has a number of credit transactions with each customer, you may be able to save bookkeeping time by accumulating each customer's sales checks and receipts in a jacket or pocket during the month instead of posting them. At the end of the month, the sales checks can be added and the adding-machine tape stapled to them and enclosed with a statement showing only the customer's balance at the end of the month. This one total is also entered on the customer's ledger sheet.

A record of some sort must be made of the details of the sales billed, however. This can be done by running a second adding-machine tape of the sales checks, recording on it the sales-check number applying to each amount, and retaining it in your files. (This will also check the addition on the statement sent to the customer.) Another method is to note each sales-check number in the description column of the customer's ledger sheet. Still another is to list each sales-check number and amount on the statement instead of enclosing the sales checks and adding-machine tape. With a small number of transactions, the sales-check number should make it possible for you to find the sales check if any question comes up after you have billed the customer.

Before You Mail the Statement: Before the statements are put in the envelopes for mailing, the ending balances shown on all statements should be totaled to make sure that the total of these balances agrees with the balance shown on the accounts-receivable control sheet. This can take the place of the end-of-the-month balancing of the *Accounts Receivable Ledger* already described. It also allows you to check not only the accuracy of the figures but the accuracy of the copying of the statements as well.

As the statements are being prepared, all customers having unpaid balances from the preceding month should be noted. A reminder of the overdue balance should be enclosed with the statements of these customers.

UNIDENTIFIED ITEMS

In Part II it was mentioned that you may occasionally have collections on account that cannot be identified because of missing or incomplete information. The *Accounts Receivable Ledger* should include a sheet headed "Unidentified Cash" to which each of these items is posted. This ledger sheet is handled like a customer's account in balancing, except that it always has a credit balance.

Recording Unidentified Payments: The customers involved will probably call your attention to the fact that they have not been

HOW TO HANDLE ERRORS IN
ACCOUNTS RECEIVABLE BALANCES

If your *Accounts Receivable Ledger* does not balance after a day's posting, total all sales posted to the customers' accounts for the day. The result should agree with the charge sales reported on the *Daily Summary*. If it does not, the difference might be due to one of the following causes:

■ incorrect amount posted to a customer's account

■ amount posted to a customer's account incorrectly added or subtracted

■ charge sales incorrectly totaled for the *Daily Summary*

■ sales check missing

Any of these errors could be located by comparing the adding-machine tape of the ledger postings with the additions of charge sales for the *Daily Summary*. Collections on account should be checked in the same way.

If after any necessary corrections the sales and cash postings agree with the *Daily Summary* but the total of the individual ledger accounts still does not agree with the control sheet, look for an error in addition on the customers' ledger sheets or the control sheet.

If the source of a discrepancy cannot be located, note the amount of the difference on the control sheet. The next time you try to balance these accounts, you may find that they still differ by the same amount. This will mean that no further error has been made. At the end of the year, differences still unsolved should be charged off by using the method described in Chapter 18 for writing off bad debts.

given credit for these payments. If a payment claimed by a customer can be identified as having been entered in the "Unidentified Cash" account, the amount is entered as a credit in the customer's account and as a debit in the "Unidentified Cash" account. It does not have to be entered in your journals nor on your accounts-receivable control sheet, but an explanation should be noted in both the customer's account and the "Unidentified Cash" account.

Recording Unidentified Charge Sales: Occasionally there may be a charge-sales check on which the salesperson neglected to enter the customer's name. If the salesperson cannot remember what customer it was, the sales check should be posted as a debit to an account headed "Unidentified Customers." It is much less likely that a customer will call your attention to a missing charge than to a missing payment, but there is a possibility that the sale might later be identified. If this happens, the customer's account is debited, and the "Unidentified Customers" account credited for the amount.

Charging Off Unidentified Items: At the end of the year, you should review the "Unidentified Cash" and "Unidentified Customers" accounts and charge off old balances that will probably never be identified. The method for doing this is described later in the discussion of writing off bad debts.

CREDIT PLANS

In many localities, there are central credit plans or services. There are also several well-known national credit-card organizations that operate in much the same manner as the local plans.

Under a typical credit plan, your customer has a card allowing him or her to deal on a credit basis with you and many other merchants in your area. You submit all sales checks from such customers to the plan at agreed-upon intervals and receive a check for the total amount less a service charge. The billing and collection functions are then taken over by the credit plan.

The plan will probably furnish you standard transmittal envelopes in which to remit your sales checks. (Unless you have a very small volume of sales, daily remittances are advisable.) The transmittal envelopes will probably provide a tally on which to total the enclosed sales checks and a space for computing the discount or service charge and showing the net amount you will receive from the plan.

Recording Credit-Plan Sales: If you are a member of a credit plan, you will not need a separate *Accounts Receivable Ledger*, since you will have only one account, an account for the plan. (If you are a member of two or more plans, of course, an account will be needed for each plan.)

As with non-credit-plan charge sales, the total of the day's charge sales is entered on the *Daily Summary* and from there to the *Sales and Cash Receipts Journal.* As each transmittal is prepared, the total of the charge sales included is posted as a debit on the accounts-receivable ledger sheet. The service charge can be recorded in a column added to the *Sales and Cash Receipts Journal.* This column will not enter into the previously described cross-checking of the journal columns, but at the end of the month, the total of the column will be posted as a credit to the "Accounts Receivable" account and as an expense item on the Profit-and-Loss Statement.

Payments received from the plan are recorded in the *Daily Summary* and *Cash Receipts Journal* like any other collection on account and posted to the credit column of the accounts-receivable ledger sheet. If a transmittal slip is corrected by the plan and as a result the amount received is not the amount you computed and entered in your records, a correcting entry should be made in the columns involved.

After all posting has been completed, the balance due from the credit plan as shown in the "Accounts Receivable" account should equal the net amount of all transmittals for which payment has not been received.

17
Aging Your Accounts Receivable

At least two or three times a year, your accounts receivable should be *aged*. To do this, make up a sheet with the following column headings: "Total Amount," "Current," "30–60 Days," "60–90 Days," "3–6 Months," "6–9 Months," "9–12 Months," and "Over 1 Year" (see Exhibit 15).

The balance of each of your accounts receivable is then entered in the "Total Amount" column. If all the charges in a given account were made in the current month, the total is also entered in the "Current" column. If the charges made in the current month do not account for the entire balance, enough of the charges made in the preceding month are entered in the "30–60 Days" column to make up the difference. If no charges were made in the preceding month, or if the charges made then are not enough to make up the difference, the charges for the next preceding month—or enough to make up the total—are entered in the "60–90 Days" column, and so on. If no charge sales were made to the customer in the time period covered by a column, no entry is made in that column, even though entries may be necessary in earlier columns.

Suppose that customer A (Exhibit 15) has a balance of $103.50 on September 30. Following is a summary of his account for the past four months:

	Debit	Credit	Balance
June...........................	51.50	....	51.50
July	....	50.00	1.50
August	49.50	....	51.00
September......................	52.50	....	103.50

On the aging schedule, his balance of $103.50 is entered in the "Total Amount" column and his September purchases of $52.50 in the "Current" column. Since all of his August purchases are needed to make up the balance, the $49.50 is entered in the "30–60 Days" column. There is still $1.50 of the total balance to be accounted for. He made no purchases on account during July, however, so no entry is made in the "60–90 Days" column. Instead, the $1.50 is entered in the "3–6 Months" column, since the $1.50 is part of the June charges.

After all the individual accounts have been aged, each column should be totaled. The total of the "Total Amount" column should equal the sum of the totals of the other columns. It should also agree with the total in the accounts-receivable control sheet.

Aging your accounts receivable brings to your attention accounts that are slow and deserve extra collection effort or suspension of credit privileges. It is also useful in comparing the overall aging of your accounts receivable for different periods. For this purpose, the percentages of the total represented by the individual columns are more useful than the dollar amounts.

EXHIBIT 15: AGING OF ACCOUNTS RECEIVABLE

Customer	Total Amount	Current	30-60 Days	60-90 Days	3-6 Months	6-9 Months	9-12 Months	Over 1 Year
A	$103.50	$52.50	$49.50		$1.50			
B	23.00	23.00						
C	9.75					$5.50	$4.25	
M	4.25	4.25						
N	45.00	29.75	15.25					
O	12.00	7.00		$5.00				
R	10.00							$10.00
S	50.00	50.00						
X	28.00	20.00	8.00					
Y	14.50				14.50			
Z	35.00	35.00						
Total	$450.00	$336.50	$72.75	$5.00	$16.00	$5.50	$4.25	$10.00
Percent	100	75	16	1	4	1	1	2

18
Accounting for Bad Debts

Any business that grants credit will sooner or later run into collection losses, or *bad debts*. Such losses may be recorded in either of two ways: by the *direct charge-off method* or by the *allowance method*.

THE DIRECT CHARGE-OFF METHOD

Under this method, when it becomes obvious that one or more accounts are uncollectible (usually determined by a periodic review of your customers' accounts), they are removed from the books, or *charged off* as follows:

1. The total of all the balances to be charged off is entered in the *Cash Disbursements, Purchases, and Expense Journal*— as a debit under "Miscellaneous Income and Expense Items," with the description "Bad debts," and as a credit under "General Ledger Items," with "Accounts receivable" shown as the account.

2. The total is also entered in the credit column of the

accounts-receivable control sheet to reduce the accounts-receivable balance by that amount.

3. The individual amounts are entered in the credit columns of the individual customer accounts. This will ordinarily reduce each of the accounts involved to zero.

Any long-standing difference between the total of the individual customer accounts and the control sheet (discussed earlier in this section) should be included in the bad-debts total entered in the journal and on the control sheet. No individual customer account is affected by this adjustment.

THE ALLOWANCE METHOD

Under the allowance method of accounting for bad-debt losses, it is assumed that some accounts will prove uncollectible. An allowance is therefore provided against which the bad accounts can be charged.

Setting Up the Allowance: The first problem is to know how much of an allowance to provide. If you have an established business, your past bad-debt losses will serve as a guide, but if you are just starting in business, you will have to make an estimate. Bad-debt losses vary greatly with the type of business, the credit and collection policies, and the economic environment in which your business operates. Your best guide to the bad debts to be expected is the experience of other businesses as similar to yours as possible. You may be able to get this information from a trade association, your suppliers, or personal acquaintances in your type of business.

After you have decided on the rate of provision for bad debts, an entry is made at the end of each month in the *Cash Disbursements, Purchases, and Expense Journal.* The description is entered as "Bad debts," and the amount of the monthly allowance is entered as a debit under "Miscellaneous Income and Expense Items" and as a credit under "General Ledger Items." The *General Ledger* entry will be posted to the account "Allowance for Bad Debts."

Periodically but in any case at the end of each year, you

should measure your allowance for bad debts against an aging of your accounts receivable. If you feel that the allowance is not large enough, an additional entry to make up the amount needed should be made; if you feel that it is already too large, an entry reversing a part of the allowance previously provided should be made. This analysis will also suggest whether you should raise or lower the monthly bad-debts entry for future periods.

Charging Off the Bad Debts: Your customer accounts should be reviewed periodically to determine which ones should be charged off. The total of these uncollectible accounts is then entered in the *Cash Disbursements Journal* under "General Ledger Items"—once as a debit, with the account described as "Allowance for bad debts," and again as a credit, with the account described as "Accounts receivable." The total is also entered in the credit column of the accounts-receivable control sheet, and the individual amounts are entered in the credit columns of the individual customer accounts.

PAYMENTS RECEIVED ON BAD DEBTS

Occasionally a collection may be received on an account after the account has been charged off as uncollectible. Such a receipt is recorded in the *Daily Summary* and in the *Cash Receipts Journal,* but not as cash received on account, since the account is no longer on the books. The entry is included in "Miscellaneous Receipts" on the *Daily Summary* and is entered in the *Cash Receipts Journal* as a credit under "General Ledger Items," with the account shown as "Allowance for bad debts." It will, of course, be in the "Total Cash Deposit."

It is possible that at the time the cash receipt is recorded, the person recording it will not realize that the account has been charged off and will record the receipt as a normal collection on account. The error will be discovered when the entry is to be posted to the customer's account. At that time, a correcting entry is made. The amount of the cash receipt is entered as a credit under "General Ledger Items," with the account shown as "Allowance for bad debts," and as a deduction in the "Collections on Account" column.

PART VIII
SOME SPECIAL CASH-RECEIPTS SITUATIONS

19
Return Sales and Refunds

In most businesses, it is sometimes necessary to accept returned merchandise for credit or refund. In some cases, refunds are made without the return of merchandise.

You should establish certain safeguards to protect yourself against unauthorized returns, returns of merchandise purchased elsewhere, or refund or credit of too great an amount. These safeguards should include the following policy rules:

1. The original cash-register slip or sales check must be presented when merchandise is returned.
2. No refunds will be made on purchases after a specified length of time.
3. No cash refunds will be made on charge purchases.
4. All returns must be made at a designated place in the store or be approved by one or more authorized persons.

TYPES OF REFUNDS

Refunds will generally be necessary because of one of the following situations:

- Return of resalable merchandise
- Return of defective or unsalable merchandise
- Refund of overcharge
- Refund for adjustment on unsatisfactory merchandise kept by customer
- Refund of deposit on returnable containers (soft-drink bottles and so on)

When salable merchandise is returned, it should be returned to stock promptly. When unsalable or defective merchandise is returned or a customer is given an adjustment for unsatisfactory merchandise, determine whether the supplier should be held responsible for the defect. If so, take steps to recover your purchase price or the amount of the adjustment from the supplier.

An even exchange in which the return merchandise is salable and the replacing merchandise comes from the same department need not be recorded. Uneven exchanges and even exchanges in which the replacing merchandise is from a different department should be treated as returns of the old items and sales of the replacing items.

RETURNS OR REFUNDS ON CHARGE SALES

In any type of return or refund on a charge sale, a credit slip should be issued to the customer. This can be a regular sales check plainly marked "Return sale" or "Credit." Or if you have enough returns to justify it, you can use special credit slips. If special credit slips are used, they should be prenumbered and controlled in the same way that charge-sales checks are.

When you add up the charge sales for the *Daily Summary*, any sales checks representing returns or refunds on charge sales are subtracted from the total. The net charge-sales figure is then entered on the summary. The return or refund sales checks should be kept with the rest of the day's charge-sales checks to be entered as credits to the individual customer accounts.

RETURNS OR REFUNDS ON CASH SALES

There are several methods of handling returns on merchandise for which the customer paid cash.

1. If you use sales checks instead of a cash register, a credit-sales check marked "Cash refund" should be made out and the cash refunded to the customer. Information taken from the original sales check should be entered on the credit slip so that the amount of the credit can be deducted from the totals of the proper department. When the cash-sales figure is prepared for the *Daily Summary,* the amount of the refund will be subtracted from the total.

2. If you use a cash register with a return-sales key, the return sale is rung up. Some cash registers subtract return sales directly from sales. In such cases, the totals in the cash register at the end of the day are net sales and can be entered on the *Daily Summary* as they are. Other cash registers show only the total returned sales, and this total must be subtracted from the cash-sales total.

3. If you do not have many return sales and refunds and they do not add up to much money, they can be treated as petty-cash payments and a petty-cash slip made out for them.

4. For large refunds, you may not want to make a cash refund from the cash register. In that case, you can issue a check to the customer for the amount of the refund. The check does not affect the *Daily Summary;* sales will be reduced when the check is recorded in the *Cash Disbursements Journal.*

REFUNDS FOR RETURNABLE CONTAINERS

Refunds of deposits on soft-drink bottles or other returnable containers are routine and usually small. They should be handled with as little recordkeeping as possible.

One way to do this is to have a special place where all such bottles or containers are to be returned. A clerk stationed nearby is given a fund large enough to take care of a normal day's refunds. In smaller stores, the bottle fund may be simply set aside in a small container.

When bottles are returned, the customer is paid, and no record is made of the payment. At the end of the day, the bottles are sorted by type and their total deposit value computed. This amount plus the remaining cash should equal the fixed amount of the fund. A memo of the total day's refunds is then given to the main cashier, who restores that amount to the bottle fund. Since the deposit, when it was collected, was treated as part of the sales price, the total of the deposits refunded during the day is deducted from the cash-sales total when the *Daily Summary* is prepared. The memo is kept with the summary.

20
Making Purchases from Cash Receipts

It is important that you (1) deposit all cash receipts, (2) make all major payments of the business by check, and (3) handle all other cash payments through a petty-cash fund. Sometimes, however, exceptions must be made to these rules. In some types of business (particularly groceries or rural general stores) it is customary to make many merchandise purchases by cash rather than by check. These purchases may be from suppliers' representatives or from farmers. If your volume of such purchases is substantial, you will not find it practical to handle them through your petty-cash fund.

The following suggestions will help you keep your records in good shape if you must make payments from cash receipts:

1. Try to confine all such payments to one type of spending (for example, merchandise purchases), and use the petty-cash fund for all other cash payments.
2. Always get a written receipt showing the vendor's name, date, a brief description of the purchase, and amount paid.

3. If you use a cash register, have a paid-out key and ring up each payment made from cash receipts. At the end of each day, balance the register's paid-out total against the total of the written receipts for the day's cash purchases. If you do not use a cash register, or if your cash register does not have a paid-out key, the receipts can be added to get the total paid-outs for the day.

4. Design your *Daily Summary* so that Item 4, "Total Receipts to Be Accounted For," is a subtotal. From this figure deduct the total of your day's paid-outs to get "Net Receipts to Be Accounted For." The "Cash Receipts" section of the *Daily Summary* will then read as follows (the rest of the form will be as shown in Exhibit 3):

Cash Sales .... $_____
Collections on Account .... _____
Miscellaneous Receipts .... _____
Total Receipts .... $_____
Less Merchandise Purchases .... _____
Net Receipts to Be Accounted For .... $_____

---

5. Design your *Sales and Cash Receipts Journal* (Exhibit 4) to conform to the *Daily Summary*. That is, provide an additional column headed "Merchandise Purchases." This column will be a debit column. The total must be included in the amount entered for purchases on the Profit-and-Loss Statement.

21
Cashing Customers' Checks

In some communities and in some types of business, checks are often cashed for quite a number of customers. To protect yourself, you should take the following precautions before accepting checks:

1. If the check is a personal check, know the person who wrote it (or the endorser presenting the check), and be reasonably certain that the individual is good for the amount of the check. In effect, you are extending credit to the endorser until the check clears the bank.
2. In the case of payroll checks, know the company, and require the endorser presenting the check to identify himself or herself as the payee.
3. Get enough information from the person presenting the check to enable you to contact him or her if you need to.

HANDLING BAD CHECKS

In spite of precautions, in almost any business in which checks are taken from customers, now and then a check will be returned by the bank as uncollectible. When this happens, contact the person from whom you accepted the check at once. Try to get that individual to replace it with cash or another check. If the check is made good in the same month, no entry is needed in your *Daily Summary* or in the *Sales and Cash Receipts Journal.* However, a new deposit slip should be prepared and your copy marked, "Replacement of [customer's name] check returned by bank on [date]."

If a returned check has not been made good by the end of the month in which it was returned, an entry should be made in your checkbook to reduce your bank balance by the amount of the check. An entry is also needed in the *Sales and Cash Receipts Journal* as follows:

1. Write the name of the customer and "Returned check" in the description column.
2. Enter the amount of the check, in red or in parentheses to show that it is a deduction, under "Total Cash Deposit."
3. If the check was originally received as a payment on account, enter the amount, in red or in parentheses, under "Collections on Account."
4. If the check was for any other purpose, enter it in the debit column under "Miscellaneous Income and Expense Items," with the account described as "Bad check."

You should go on trying to collect the check. If you succeed in collecting it in a later month, the collection is recorded among the cash receipts on the *Daily Summary*—as a collection on account if the original check was a payment on account, otherwise as a miscellaneous receipt to be entered in the *Sales and Cash Receipts Journal* as a credit under "Miscellaneous Income and Expense Items." In other words, the entries made at the time the new check is deposited reverse the entries made when the check was returned.

WHEN MANY CHECKS ARE CASHED

Some businesses cash so many checks for customers that the money taken in from other customers is not enough to take care of the check cashing. As a result, the change fund has to be larger than would otherwise be necessary.

In such circumstances, so many checks may be cashed for customers that the coins and bills at the end of the day are not enough to bring the change fund up to the fixed amount for the next day. If this happens in your business, all the checks should be deposited, but to do this and at the same time restore the change fund to its fixed amount will require some changes in your bookkeeping setup.

Changes in the *Daily Summary* Form: Your *Daily Summary* form will have to be a little different from the one shown in Exhibit 3. You will need to make the following changes in the form:

- Change the wording of Item 9, "Total Cash Deposit," to "Receipts to Be Deposited." This is still the item that should equal Item 4, "Total Receipts to Be Accounted For," and on which cash short or over will be based.
- Add Item 9a, "Excess Checks [Cash[1]] to Be Deposited."
- Add Item 9b, "Total Cash Deposit."

[1]There may be excess cash to deposit if the change fund is being reduced. This will be explained later in the chapter.

Item 9a will be the amount by which the checks (shown in Item 5) exceed the receipts to be deposited (Item 9). Item 9b will be the sum of Items 9 and 9a and should be the same as the amount of the checks (Item 5). On days when the receipts to be deposited total more than the checks cashed, Item 9a will not be used, and Item 9b will be the same as Item 9.

Changes in the *Cash Receipts Journal:*   When you enter the *Daily Summary* in the *Sales and Cash Receipts Journal,* Item 9b is entered under "Total Cash Deposit." An additional credit column headed "Exchange" is provided and the amount of the excess checks entered there. If the checks cashed for customers exceed the receipts to be deposited on only one or two days a month, a credit entry in the "General Ledger" column, with "Exchange" written in the description column, can be used instead of an additional column.

Exhibit 16 shows how your *Daily Summary* will look if the checks you cash for customers total more than the day's total receipts. Illustration II in Exhibit 4 shows the journal entries for this summary. The check to restore the change fund will be drawn for $18.00 in the illustration.

Restoring the Change Fund: To restore the change fund, when you deposit the checks at the bank cash a check drawn on your own account to "Petty cash" for the amount of the excess checks. The money is put into the change fund to bring the fund up to its fixed amount. The check will be entered in the "General Ledger" debit column of the *Cash Disbursements Journal* with the account shown as "Exchange." This entry will cancel the "Exchange" entry made in the *Cash Receipts Journal.*

Increasing and Decreasing the Change Fund: There may be only a few days each month when, because of paydays at large companies in your locality, you expect to do a large amount of check cashing for your customers. If that is the case you do not need to carry the larger change fund all the time. You can increase the fund temporarily by drawing a petty-cash check for the amount of the increase and cashing it at the bank on the day you expect to need a larger change fund. This check will be entered in the *Cash Disbursements Journal* as a debit under "General Ledger Items," with the account shown as "Exchange." Be careful, while the fund is increased, to take the proper amount of the fund into account in balancing the day's cash.

When you no longer need the extra cash, you can return the fund to its normal amount as follows:

1. If the excess checks you would otherwise enter as Item 9a on the *Daily Summary* are less than the temporary increase

EXHIBIT 16: THE *DAILY SUMMARY OF SALES AND CASH RECEIPTS* WITH EXCESS CHECKS ENTRY

DAILY SUMMARY OF SALES AND CASH RECEIPTS

Date <u>MARCH 23, 19—</u>

CASH RECEIPTS

1. Cash Sales	$435.00
2. Collections on Account	100.00
3. Miscellaneous Receipts[1]	15.00
4. Total Receipts to Be Accounted For	$550.00

CASH ON HAND

5. Cash in Register:

Coins	$ 25.00
Bills	43.00
Checks	562.00
Total Cash in Register	$630.00
6. Petty-Cash Slips	14.00
7. Total Cash Accounted For	$644.00

8. Less Change and Petty-Cash Fund:

Petty-Cash Slips	$ 14.00
Coins and Bills	86.00
Change and Petty-Cash Fund [fixed amount]	100.00
9. Receipts to Be Deposited	$544.00
9a. Excess Checks to Be Deposited	18.00
9b. Total Cash Deposit	$562.00
10. Cash Short (Item 4 less Item 9 if Item 4 is larger)	$ 6.00
11. Cash Over (Item 9 less Item 4 if Item 9 is larger)	—

TOTAL SALES

12. Cash Sales	$435.00
13. Charge Sales (sales checks #262 to #316)	225.00
14. Total Sales	$660.00

by <u>John Doe</u>

[1]Note to appear on back of summary: "Miscellaneous receipts: Refund on merchandise $15.00."

in the fund, enter the amount of the temporary increase, instead of the amount of the excess checks, as Item 9a.

2. If the excess checks entered as Item 9a total more than the temporary increase in the fund, reduce the petty-cash check drawn for that day by the amount of the temporary increase in the fund.

In either case, follow the instructions in Part III for entering the *Daily Summary* and the petty-cash check in the journals. This will result in credits and debits to "Exchange" that will exactly offset the entry in the *Cash Disbursements Journal* made when the check to increase the fund was drawn.

22
Redeeming Coupons

More and more often, manufacturers are offering coupons that can be used as part payment on certain products. The merchant who redeems the coupons sends them to the manufacturer or manufacturer's representative and receives cash for them in the amount of the coupons, usually plus a certain amount for the trouble of handling them.

If you redeem many of these coupons, they should be treated like cash when they are received from the customer. The entire amount of the sale is recorded or rung up and the coupons put in the cash register, along with the actual money paid by the customer.

RECORDING THE COUPONS

When you balance the day's work, these coupons are treated as petty-cash slips and are included in the amount entered on the *Daily Summary* for petty-cash slips. They can be included in the petty-cash check used to restore the fund, or a special check can be made for the amount of the coupons alone. In either case, when the check is drawn, the coupons are sent to the manufacturer (or manufacturers), and the amount of the coupons is recorded as an account receivable.

A short letter should be sent with the coupons stating the number and type of coupons enclosed, their total face value, and the total amount due you, including the handling charges. A photocopy of the letter should be kept in case you need to follow up on it.

When you receive the check from the manufacturer, the face value of the coupons is recorded as a collection on account. The handling charges are treated as a miscellaneous receipt on the *Daily Summary* and entered in the *Sales and Cash Receipts Journal* as a credit under "Miscellaneous Income and Expense Items."

WHEN THE AMOUNTS ARE VERY SMALL

If the coupons sent to any one manufacturer represent a very small amount, some recordkeeping can be avoided by making out a petty-cash slip for the coupons at the time they are sent to the manufacturer. This petty-cash slip is left in the petty-cash fund until the check is received from the manufacturer. It is not included in any checks written in the meantime to restore the fund.

When the check is received, only the handling charge is recorded. The petty-cash slip is destroyed, since it is offset by the balance of the check from the manufacturer. In effect, the petty-cash slip is like an IOU from the manufacturer for the time it remains in the petty-cash fund.

PART IX
DEPRECIATION AND
DISPOSAL OF PLANT ASSETS

23
Computing Depreciation of Property and Equipment

Whatever type of business you are in, you will have to purchase property and equipment from time to time. This property will usually last for several years, so it would not be realistic to consider the whole cost an expense in any one year. Therefore, when the property is purchased, it is set upon the books as a *fixed*, or *plant, asset*. The decrease in value over the life of the property, known as *depreciation*, is treated as an expense distributed over the period during which the asset is used.

If you buy business property that has a useful life of more than one year, you may be able to deduct a limited amount of the cost as an expense when you figure your business income for tax purposes. The remainder of the cost of this property must be spread over more than one year and deducted a part at a time. Because depreciation systems may change through congressional legislation, always refer to the latest Publication 534 from the IRS.

WHAT CAN BE DEPRECIATED

Depreciable property is property for which a depreciation deduction is allowed. Many different kinds of property can be depreciated, such as machinery, buildings, and equipment. Depreciable property can be *tangible* or *intangible*. Tangible property is any property that can be seen or touched and can be divided into *real* and *personal* property. Personal property is property such as machinery, vehicles, or equipment that is not real estate. Real property is land and generally anything that is erected on, growing on, or attached to land. (Note, however, that land is never depreciable.)

Property is depreciable if it meets these requirements:

1. It must be used in business or held for the production of income.
2. It must have a determinable life of longer than one year.
3. It must be something that wears out, decays, gets used up, becomes obsolete, or loses value from natural causes.

In general, if property does not meet all three of these conditions, it is not depreciable.

MACRS AND ACRS METHODS

The depreciation method used depends on when the property was placed in service. Tangible assets placed in service after 1986 are depreciated using the *Modified Accelerated Cost Recovery System (MACRS)*. The *Accelerated Cost Recovery System (ACRS)* applies to tangible assets placed in service after 1980 and before 1987. Other methods require you to make determinations on matters such as useful life and salvage value. Under MACRS and ACRS, salvage value and useful life are not relevant.

MACRS

To calculate the annual MACRS depreciation you need to know

1. the depreciable basis of the property
2. when the property is placed in service for depreciation
3. the property class
4. which convention applies to the property
5. which MACRS method you want to use to recover your basis in the property

Each of these is briefly discussed below. (For detailed information on MACRS see IRS Publication 534.)

Basis: To deduct the proper amount of depreciation you must first determine your basis in the depreciable property—generally the original purchase price of the property. (Publication 551 explains how to calculate your basis if you acquire property in a way other than by purchase.)

Placed in Service: For depreciation, property is considered placed in service when it is ready and available for its specified use.

Property Classes: Each piece of property depreciated under MACRS is assigned to a property class. These classes establish the number of years over which the basis of the property in the class is recovered. This period of time is called a *recovery period*. Under MACRS, tangible property you place in service after 1986 falls into one of eight classes. The following is a list of property classes and examples of the property included in each. (For a more detailed list see IRS Publication 534.)

- 3-year property—tractor units for use over the road, race horses over two years old, and other horses over twelve years old
- 5-year property—automobiles, taxis, buses, trucks, computers and peripheral equipment, office machinery, and property used in research and experimentation

■ 7-year property—office furniture and fixtures and any property that does not have a class life and that has not been designated by law as being in any other class

■ 10-year property—vessels, barges, tugs, similar water-transportation equipment, any single-purpose agricultural or horticultural structure, and any tree or vine bearing fruits or nuts

■ 15-year property—roads, shrubbery, wharves, and any municipal waste-water treatment plant

■ 20-year property—farm buildings and any municipal sewers

■ Nonresidential real property—any real property that is not residential rental property (see below) and any real property that is section 1250 property with a class life of 27.5 years or more. (See Chapter 4 of IRS Publication 544 for more information on section 1250 property.) This property is depreciated over 31.5 years.

■ Residential rental property—any real property that is a rental building or structure for which 80 percent or more of the gross rental income for the tax year is rental income from dwelling units. This property is depreciated over 27.5 years.

Conventions: The convention refers to what time in the taxable year the property is assumed to be placed in service. Refer to Publication 534 on whether a half-year convention, mid-quarter convention, or mid-month convention is appropriate.

Depreciation Methods: Under MACRS, there are four ways you can recover the depreciable basis of your property:

1. *MACRS method.* For property in the 3- ,5- ,7- , or 10-year class use the double (200 percent) declining-balance method over 3- ,5- ,7- , or 10 years. For property in the 15- or 20-year class, use the 150 percent declining-balance method over 15 or 20 years. For these classes of property, change to the straight-line method for the first tax year for which that method, when applied to the adjusted basis at the beginning of the year, will yield a larger deduction. Always use the

straight-line method for nonresidential, real, and residential rental property. (For a discussion of the 200 percent and 150 percent declining-balance methods and the straight-line method, see "Other Depreciation Methods" later in this chapter.)

2. *Straight-line election.* You can elect to use the straight-line method over the recovery period. Once made, the election cannot be changed and when made for one item in a property class applies to all property in that class placed in service in the tax year of the election.

3. *150 percent election.* You may elect to use the 150 percent declining-balance method over the alternate MACRS recovery period (see below). Again, once the method is elected it cannot be changed and when made for one item in a property class applies to all property in that class placed in service in the tax year of the election.

4. *Alternate MACRS method.* To be used for tangible property predominantly outside the United States, any tax-exempt use property, any property to the extent it is financed by an obligation whose interest is exempt from federal tax, and certain imported property. In addition, you may elect to use the alternate MACRS method for most other property. Under this method depreciation is calculated using a straight-line method over the alternate recovery period. (See IRS Publication 534 for a discussion of alternate recovery periods.)

FIGURING MACRS DEDUCTION

After you know the depreciable basis of the property, the date it was placed in service, the property class, the applicable convention, and the MACRS depreciation method, you can calculate the depreciation deduction. You can figure the deduction by either referring to the MACRS depreciation tables in IRS Publication 534 or computing the deduction using the applicable depreciation method and convention over the recovery period.

ACRS

ACRS allows you to recover the unadjusted basis of recovery property over a recovery period. Your property's recovery period is determined by its *class life*. Generally the class life of property places it in a 3-year, 5-year, 10-year, 15-year, or 18-year class. A recovery percentage for each year of the recovery period is prescribed for figuring your ACRS deduction. The deduction is figured by multiplying your unadjusted basis in the property by the applicable recovery percentage. (For detailed information on ACRS see IRS Publication 534.)

Recovery Property: Recovery property is tangible, depreciable property that was placed in service after 1980 and that is not excluded property. It usually includes new or used property acquired after 1980 for use in trade or business or to be held for the production of income. Property acquired and used for any purpose before 1981 is not recovery property.

Unadjusted Basis: The ACRS deduction is figured by multiplying the unadjusted basis in recovery property by its applicable percentage for the year. Salvage value is disregarded under ACRS. The unadjusted basis may not be reduced by any salvage value when figuring deductions under ACRS.

Recovery Periods: Each item of recovery property is assigned to a class of property. These classes of recovery property establish the recovery periods over which the unadjusted basis of items in a class are recovered. The six classes with examples of inclusive property are:

1. 3-year property (automobile and light-duty trucks)
2. 5-year property (office furniture and fixtures)
3. 10-year property (manufactured homes)
4. 15-year real property (real property placed in service before March 16, 1984)
5. low-income housing
6. 18-year real property (real property placed in service after March 15, 1984)

Classes of Recovery Property: The class to which an item of recovery property is assigned is determined in part by whether it is section 1245 or section 1250 class property.

Section 1245 class property is any depreciable property that is:

1. tangible personal property
2. a special-purpose structure or storage facility that is also depreciable tangible property. (A building or its structural components may not be included. The facility must be an integral part of certain business activity, such as a research facility used in connection with this activity or a bulk storage facility for replaceable commodities used in connection with this activity. Such an activity includes manufacturing, production, extraction, or the furnishing of transportation, communications, energy, water, or sewage disposal services.)
3. a single-purpose agricultural (livestock) or horticultural structure
4. a storage facility (other than a building or its structural components) used in connection with the distribution of petroleum or any primary product of petroleum

Section 1250 class property is all depreciable real property not classified as section 1245 property or an elevator or an escalator.

Excluded Property: ACRS may not be used for certain property placed in service before 1981 but transferred after 1980. Owners may elect to exclude certain property from the application of ACRS.

Election to Exclude Certain Property: If you depreciate property under a method of depreciation not based on a term of years, such as the unit-of-production method, you may elect to exclude that property from ACRS. A depreciation deduction under the unit-of-production method is figured by dividing the cost or other basis (less salvage) by the estimated number of units to be produced during the life of the asset. The resulting amount is applied to the units produced in a year to arrive at the depreciation for that year.

Dispositions: Gain or loss from an asset is usually recognized on its disposition or retirement. Nonrecognition rules may, however, allow the postponement of some gain. (See IRS Publication 544, *Sales and Other Dispositions of Assets*.)

OTHER DEPRECIATION METHODS

Before MACRS and ACRS were enacted, other methods were used to figure depreciation. If property was placed in service before 1981, or if the property does not qualify for MACRS or ACRS, these methods must be used. However, these methods may not be used for property that qualifies for MACRS and ACRS.

There are many different methods of figuring depreciation. Any method that is reasonable may be used if it is applied consistently. Discussed next are several methods that you may be using.

Straight-Line Method: The simplest method of computing depreciation is known as the *straight-line method*. Under this method, the estimated salvage value and any additional first-year depreciation taken are subtracted from the cost. The remainder is divided by the estimated useful life of the asset. The resulting figure is the amount to be charged off as depreciation each accounting period.

For example, assume that a piece of equipment is bought for $100,000. Its salvage value is estimated at $4,000, its useful life at 12 years. If the straight-line method of depreciation is used, the annual depreciation will be computed as follows:

$$\frac{\$100,000 - \$4,000}{12} = \$8,000$$

If in the first year you use the property for less than a full year, your depreciation must be prorated for the months in use.

Sum-of-the-Years-Digits Method: The *sum-of-the-years-digits method* and the *declining-balance method* are based on the assumption that an asset depreciates faster in the early years of its life than in the later years. The total depreciation that may be charged off is the same as under the straight-line method, but some of it may be charged off sooner.

In the sum-of-the-years-digits method, the depreciation rate of an asset for any year is a fraction whose numerator is the remaining years of life of the asset (at the beginning of the year) and whose denominator is the sum of the numerators. For an asset with a four-year life, for example, the sum-of-the-years-digits method would give the following depreciation rates:

Year	Remaining life at beginning of year	Rate for the year
1	4	$\frac{4}{10}$ or 40 percent
2	3	$\frac{3}{10}$ or 30 percent
3	2	$\frac{2}{10}$ or 20 percent
4	1	$\frac{1}{10}$ or 10 percent
Total	10	$\frac{10}{10}$ or 100 percent

As in the straight-line method, these rates are applied to the cost minus the salvage value and minus any additional first-year depreciation taken.

Declining-Balance Method: For certain types of property, the declining-balance method allows the use of a speeded-up rate of depreciation. The rate may be one and one-half times or one and one-quarter times the straight-line rate, depending on the types of property.

In order to calculate the depreciation rate under the declining-balance method, begin by dividing the number 1 by the property's useful life. For example, if property has a useful life of 5 years, its normal straight-line rate of depreciation is 1/5, or 20 percent. This straight-line rate must then be multiplied by 1.5 or 1.25 (depending on the kind of property you are depreciating) to determine the declining-balance rate.

Salvage Value: Salvage value is not subtracted from your basis when figuring yearly depreciation deductions under the declining-balance method. However, the property may not be depreciated below its reasonable salvage value.

One and One-Half Times the Straight-Line Rate: Under the declining-balance method, a rate of depreciation equal to 150 percent of the straight-line rate may be used for certain types of property. To use this rate, the property must be used tangible property (used section 1245 property other than MACRS or ACRS recovery property) with a useful life of 3 years or more.

One and One-Fourth Times the Straight-Line Rate: Under the declining-balance method, a rate of depreciation of 125 percent of the straight-line rate may be used for certain used residential rental property. To qualify, the property must have a useful life of 20 years or more. For used residential rental property acquired after 1980 and before 1987, it must be property that is not ACRS property. If acquired after 1986, it must be depreciated under MACRS.

Depreciation Deductions: After determining the rate of depreciation, multiply the adjusted basis of the property by the rate. The answer is the amount of your deduction. For example, if the adjusted basis at the beginning of the first year is $10,000 and the rate is 20 percent, the depreciation deduction for the first year would be $2,000 (20% × $10,000 = $2,000). To figure the depreciation deduction for the second year, first adjust your basis for the amount of depreciation deducted in the first year. Subtract the previous year's depreciation from the basis ($10,000 − $2,000 = $8,000). Multiply this amount by the rate of depreciation ($8,000 × 20% = $1,600). Your depreciation deduction for the second year is $1,600. Each year the balance (adjusted basis in the property) gets smaller under this method, so deductions are larger in the earlier years and smaller in the later years.

24
Accounting for Depreciable Property

Property used in your trade or business is generally referred to as an asset. The cost or other basis of every asset that can be depreciated is recorded in an asset account. An owner may set up as many accounts for depreciable property as desired. Each asset may be listed separately, or two or more assets may be combined into one account.

This section contains general recordkeeping information and basically applies only to methods other than MACRS and ACRS.

SINGLE-ITEM ACCOUNTS

Under this accounting practice, each individual item of property is treated as a separate account. Under MACRS and ACRS, single-item accounts would be appropriate for all items of recovery property.

COMPONENT ACCOUNTS

Account for depreciable property (other than MACRS and ACRS recovery property) by treating each component or part of the property as a separate account.

MULTIPLE-ASSET ACCOUNTS

This method combines a number of assets with the same or different useful lives into one account, using a single rate of depreciation for the entire account. Multiple-asset accounts are generally broken down into group, classified, and composite accounts.

For MACRS and ACRS recovery property, group items by class (3-year, 5-year, etc.) for the year placed in service, except for nonresidential real property and residential rental property under MACRS and 15-year real property under ACRS, which may be grouped by month and year placed in service.

RESERVE FOR DEPRECIATION

Figure depreciation allowances separately for each account, and record the depreciation for each in a separate depreciation reserve account.

MACRS AND ACRS DEDUCTION ACCOUNTS

Record the MACRS and ACRS deductions for recovery property in accounts that show the MACRS and ACRS deductions claimed either by class or on a property-by-property basis.

DISPOSITION OF ASSETS

A *disposition* is the permanent withdrawal of property from use in your trade or business or in the production of income. A withdrawal can be made by sale, exchange, retirement, abandonment, or destruction.

You generally recognize gain or loss on the disposition of an asset by sale. Nonrecognition rules may allow you to postpone some gain. See IRS Publication 544 for more detailed information on the treatment required in the disposition of assets.

If property is disposed of before the end of its recovery period, it is referred to as an *early disposition*. If you dispose of property depreciated under MACRS, you are allowed a depreciation deduction in the year of disposition (this is not the case, however, for property depreciated under ACRS).

25
Recording the Purchase and Depreciation of Plant Assets

What follows is a detailed description of recording the purchase and depreciation of plant assets that assumes the straight-line method was used when the assets were purchased. This information is included, although the MACRS method is currently required by the federal government, because in some states MACRS is not accepted for reporting taxes.

Generally a separate account is set up in the *General Ledger* for each major class of property, such as furniture and fixtures, delivery equipment, buildings, and leasehold improvements. Sometimes, however, more than one depreciation rate or method is applied to different items in one class of equipment. When that happens, separate accounts should be set up for the property to which each rate or method is applied. These separate accounts may be either in the *General Ledger* or in subsidiary accounts that are summarized in a *General Ledger* account.

RECORDING THE PURCHASE

If equipment is purchased for cash or on an account to be paid in a short time, the entry is made in the *Cash Disbursements, Purchases, and Expense Journal* at the time payment is made.

The amount will be entered in the "Amount of Check" column and in the "General Ledger" debit column, with the account shown as the name of the asset purchased.

Often equipment is purchased with a down payment and a note for the balance payable over a number of months or years. In this case, the down payment is entered in the "Amount of Check" column; the unpaid balance as a credit under "General Ledger Items," with the account shown as "Notes payable"; and the total cost as a debit under "General Ledger Items," with the name of the asset purchased shown as the account. Interest should not be included in the cost of the equipment; it should be treated as an expense when it is paid.

As payments are made on the note, the amount of the payment is entered (1) in the "Amount of Check" column and (2) as a debit in the "General Ledger" column, with the account shown as "Notes payable." If part of the payment applies to interest, this amount is entered as a debit under "Miscellaneous Income and Expense Items," and the remainder is debited to "Notes payable" in the "General Ledger" column.

An Example: Suppose you purchase a counter for $700. You make a down payment of $100 and sign a note for the balance at 6 percent per year, to be paid at the rate of $100 a month. The entries in the *Cash Disbursements Journal* for the purchase and the first payment on the note will be as follows:

Transaction	Description or account	Column	Amount
Purchase	Furniture and fixtures	General Ledger Items (DR.)	$700
		Amount of Check (CR.)	100
	Notes payable	General Ledger Items (CR.)	600
First Payment	Notes payable	Amount of Check (CR.)	$103
		General Ledger Items (DR.)	100
	Interest	Miscellaneous Income and Expense Items (DR.)	3

Purchase of a Going Business: If you buy a going business for a lump sum, the amount paid may not be the same as the value of the business shown on the books of the former owner. This creates the problem of distributing the purchase price among the various assets purchased. To avoid income-tax problems, you should consult an accountant or other qualified tax practitioner before recording the transaction in your books.

DEPRECIATION SCHEDULES

Depreciation can be computed separately for each item of property in your business. It is simpler, however, and usually just as satisfactory to group all items of a given class (equipment, machinery, buildings, etc.) for which the same method of depreciation is used and estimate an average rate of depreciation for each group.

A *depreciation schedule* should be set up for each group of assets and each method of depreciation used. Exhibit 17 is an example of a depreciation schedule for delivery trucks that are depreciated on a straight-line basis.

The first two dollar columns of this schedule show the cost of the assets and the accumulated allowance for depreciation. Each of the other columns except the last provides for scheduling one year's depreciation. The last column is used for the salvage value and the balance that will remain after the last year for which there is room on the schedule. The balance and the salvage value are carried forward to the next sheet.

At the end of each year, equipment or other depreciable property purchased during the year is recorded on the proper depreciation schedule. The probable depreciation will have to be computed in the meantime for your monthly statements; but you may not want to make some decisions final (what method of depreciation to use, whether to take additional first-year depreciation, and so on) until you know what the year's profit picture is going to be. Any difference between the estimated and actual depreciation for the year can be adjusted when the final month's entry is made.

EXHIBIT 17: A DEPRECIATION SCHEDULE

Date	Cost	Allowance for Depreciation	1970	1971	1972	1973	1974	1975	1976	Remaining Balance
1970 (Salvage value $500)	4500 00	400 00	400 00	800 00	800 00	800 00	800 00	400 00	(Salv)	500 00
Balance 12-31-70	4500 00	400 00								
1971		800 00								
Balance 12-31-71	4500 00	1200 00								
1972		800 00								
Balance 12-31-72	4500 00	2000 00								
1973 (Salvage value $500)	5400 00	1290 00				490 00	980 00	980 00	980 00	1470 00
Balance 12-31-73	9900 00	3290 00				1290 00				500 00
7-1-74 Disposal of 1970 truck	(4500 00)	(3200 00)					(400 00)	(400 00)		(500 00)
1974		1380 00					1380 00			
Balance 12-31-74	5400 00	1470 00								

To record the purchase of equipment on the depreciation schedule, enter the salvage value in the description column and the cost in the "Cost" column. Then compute the annual depreciation for that purchase and distribute it, with the salvage value, in the years' and "Remaining Balance" columns.

Whether or not any equipment has been purchased during the year, at the end of each year all depreciation for the year is transferred, or closed, into the "Allowance" column. At all times, the "Allowance" column plus all "open" years' depreciation plus the total of the "Remaining Balance" column should equal the total of the "Cost" column.

Thus, in Exhibit 17 at the end of 1974 the figures should be checked in the following manner:

$$1470 + (400 + 980 - 400) + 980 + (500 + 1470 + 500 - 500) = 5400$$

The totals of the "Cost" and "Allowance" columns should equal the balances of the corresponding accounts in the *General Ledger* as of the end of the year.

Theoretically depreciation of each addition to the "Cost" column for the year of purchase should be computed on the basis of the remaining months of the year. You will find it much simpler, however, to use an average of six months' depreciation. Income-tax regulations do not specifically provide for this method, but the IRS allows it if it is used consistently and does not result in a gross overstatement of depreciation in any one year.

An Example: In Exhibit 17, it is assumed that the business opened in 1970. A truck was purchased at that time for $4,500 and another one three years later, in 1973, for $5,400. Thus, the 12-31-73 "Cost" and accumulated-depreciation balances include both trucks. Then, since the older truck is disposed of in 1974, the 12-31-74 balances include only the truck purchased in 1973.

In each case, the salvage value was estimated at $500, and the useful life of the equipment at five years. Depreciation is computed by the straight-line method. For the truck purchased in 1970, this means that $4,000 is to be depreciated at an annual rate of ⅕ of $4,000, or $800. Allowing six months' depreciation, or $400, for the first year leaves $400 to be depreciated in 1975.

The truck purchased in 1973 is depreciated at the rate of $980 a year. Again, six months' depreciation is charged in the first and last years. The salvage value will remain on the schedule until the truck is disposed of.

RECORDING THE
DEPRECIATION IN YOUR BOOKS

Although depreciation is computed on an annual basis, you need to know each month's depreciation for use in preparing monthly financial statements. For assets on hand at the beginning of the year, the monthly depreciation can be computed from the depreciation schedules simply by dividing the total depreciation scheduled for that year by twelve. When additional property is purchased during the year, the year's depreciation on it should be estimated, and from this figure the depreciation for the month. The total monthly depreciation is then increased by this amount.

For example, in Exhibit 17, at the beginning of 1973, you know there will be a year's depreciation of $800.00 on the truck then on hand. You will therefore have monthly depreciation on this truck of $800 ÷ 12, or $66.67. In March 1973, you buy the second truck. At that time, you estimate that you will have depreciation in 1973 of $490.00 on the new truck. This amount will be recorded ¹⁄₁₀, or $49.00, in each of the months from March to December. Your total depreciation for each of these months will therefore be $66.67 + $49.00, or $115.67. Total depreciation for the year 1973 will thus agree with Exhibit 17:

Two months (January and February) at $66.67 . . . . $ 133.34
Ten months (March through November at $115.67;
    December $115.63 to adjust for fractions). 1,156.66

Total for the year $1,290.00

As explained earlier, the new truck will not be entered on the depreciation schedule until the end of the year. It is possible that you may decide then to use a different method of computing depreciation from the one you used in recording the estimated monthly depreciation. If that happens, you should adjust the final month's depreciation entry in your books so that the year's total will be equal to the depreciation shown for the year on the schedule.

The monthly depreciation is entered in your *Cash Disbursements, Purchases, and Expense Journal*—as a debit in the "Miscellaneous Income and Expense Items" column, with the account shown as "Depreciation," and as a credit in the "General Ledger" column, with the account shown as "Allowance for depreciation of [name of asset account]."

In recording property and depreciation, it is important that your books be kept strictly in accordance with federal income-tax requirements. If you are doing business in a state whose requirements differ from the federal requirements, you may have to keep separate property records for state-tax purposes.

IRS Publication 534 is a useful guide to the handling of depreciation from the standpoint of federal income-tax regulations.

26
Recording the Retirement of Plant Assets

Below is a detailed description of the retirement of plant assets as it was done in the past. This information is included although the MACRS method is currently required by the federal government, because in some states MACRS is not accepted for reporting taxes.

The salvage value of a fully depreciated asset remains on the depreciation schedule, and the cost and accumulated allowance for depreciation remain in the *General Ledger* accounts, until the asset is disposed of. Disposal of an asset will be one of the following:

- Sale of a fully depreciated asset
- Sale of an asset that still has *book value* (the undepreciated balance of an asset, or the original cost less the accumulated depreciation)
- Trade-in of a fully depreciated asset
- Trade-in of an asset that still has book value
- Junking of a fully depreciated asset
- Junking of an asset that still has book value

The entries necessary for each of these types of disposal are explained below and tabulated in Exhibit 18 on pages 140–141.

SALE OF A FULLY DEPRECIATED ASSET

When a fully depreciated asset is sold, whatever amount you receive is a gain and should be recorded as such. This is done by entering the amount received from the *Daily Summary* ("Miscellaneous Receipts") to the "Total Cash Deposit" column of the *Sales and Cash Receipts Journal* and to the credit column under "Miscellaneous Income and Expense Items," with the account shown as "Gain or loss on disposal of assets."

Entries must also be made to remove the cost of the asset and the allowance for depreciation from the *General Ledger*. This is done by making two offsetting entries for the amount of the asset's cost in the "General Ledger" columns of the journal. A credit entry is made with the account shown as the proper asset account, for example, "Furniture and fixtures." The other entry is a debit with the account shown as "Allowance for depreciation of furniture and fixtures" (or whatever type of asset has been sold).

SALE OF AN ASSET WITH BOOK VALUE

The sale of an asset that has an undepreciated balance on the books can result in either a gain or a loss. It depends upon whether you sell it for more or less than the undepreciated balance. If there is a gain, the following entries are made in the *Sales and Cash Receipts Journal:*

- Enter the amount received from the *Daily Summary* to the "Total Cash Deposit" column.
- Enter the gain (cash received less book value) in the "Miscellaneous Income and Expense Items" credit column, with the account shown as "Gain or loss on disposal of assets."
- Enter the cost of the asset in the "General Ledger Items" credit column with the asset account shown.

■ Enter the accumulated allowance for depreciation in the "General Ledger" debit column, with the account shown as "Allowance for depreciation of [name of asset account]."

If the sale results in a loss, the entries are the same except for the second one, which will be as follows:

■ Enter the loss (book value less cash received) in the "Miscellaneous Income and Expense Items" debit column, with the account shown as "Gain or loss on disposal of assets."

TRADE-IN OF AN ASSET

The IRS does not recognize any gain or loss from the trade-in of an asset. If the asset traded in still has book value, this book value is considered as part of the cost of the new asset. Thus, the cost basis of the new asset becomes the cash actually paid for it plus the book value of the asset traded. No recognition is given to any trade-in allowance agreed upon by you and the vendor.

Trade-In of an Asset with Book Value: Assume that an adding machine is purchased for $350.00 with a $50.00 allowance for trade-in of an old adding machine. This leaves a net cash payment of $300.00. The old adding machine was purchased for $250.00, and allowance for its depreciation totaled $212.50 by the date of the trade-in, leaving a book value of $37.50. The new machine will thus have a cost basis of $337.50 ($300.00 cash plus the $37.50 book value of the old machine).

   Since there is already $250.00 in the asset account, another $87.50 must be added to bring it up to the $337.50 cost of the new machine. Also, since there is no depreciation on the new machine as yet, the $212.50 depreciation on the old machine must be removed from the "Allowance for Depreciation" account. The entry in the *Cash Disbursements, Purchases, and Expense Journal* is therefore as follows:

■ $300 in the "Amount of Check" column

EXHIBIT 18: ENTRIES FOR RECORDING DISPOSAL OF PLANT ASSETS

Transaction	Account to be entered	Account shown as	Column in which amount is entered
Sale of fully depreciated asset	Amount of cash received	Gain or loss on disposal of assets	Total Cash Deposit, and Miscellaneous Income and Expense (credit)
	Cost of the asset	[Name of asset account]	General Ledger (credit)
	Cost of the asset	Allowance for depreciation of [name of asset account]	General Ledger (credit)
Sale of asset with book value	Cost of the asset	[Name of asset account]	General Ledger (credit)
	Difference between cash received and book value	Gain or loss on disposal of assets	Miscellaneous Income and Expense (credit if cash received is more than book value; debit if less)
	Amount of each cash received		Total Cash Deposit
	Accumulated allowance for depreciation	Allowance for depreciation of [name of asset account]	General Ledger (debit)

Transaction	Amount	Account	Entry
Trade-in of fully depreciated asset	Cash paid for new asset	[Name of payee]	Amount of Check
	Difference between cash paid and cost of old asset	[Name of asset account]	General Ledger (debit if cash paid is more than cost of old asset; credit if less)
	Cost of old asset	Allowance for depreciation of [name of asset account]	General Ledger (debit)
Trade-in of asset with book value	Cash paid for new asset	[Name of payee]	Amount of Check
	Difference between cost of new asset (cash paid + book value of old asset) and original cost of old asset	[Name of asset account]	General Ledger (debit if cost of new asset is more than cost of old asset; credit if less)
	Accumulated allowance for depreciation	Allowance for depreciation of [name of asset account]	General Ledger (debit)
Junking of fully depreciated asset	Cost of the asset	Allowance for depreciation of [name of asset account]	General Ledger (debit)
	Cost of the asset	[Name of asset account]	General Ledger (credit)
Junking of asset with book value	Book value of the asset	Loss on abandonment of property	Miscellaneous Income and Expense (debit)
	Cost of the asset	[Name of asset account]	General Ledger (credit)
	Accumulated allowance for depreciation	Allowance for depreciation of [name of asset account]	General Ledger (debit)

- $87.50 in the "General Ledger" debit column, with the account shown as "Furniture and fixtures"
- $212.50 in the "General Ledger" debit column, with the account shown as "Allowance for depreciation—furniture and fixtures"

Trade-In of a Fully Depreciated Asset: If the machine traded in had been fully depreciated and therefore had no book value, the cost basis for the new machine would be simply the $300.00 cash paid. The entries would be as follows:

- $300.00 in the "Amount of Check" column
- $50.00 in the "General Ledger" debit column, with the account shown as "Furniture and fixtures"
- $250.00 in the "General Ledger" debit column, with the account shown as "Allowance for depreciation—furniture and fixtures"

JUNKING OF AN ASSET

The junking of an asset is recorded through the *Cash Disbursements, Purchases, and Expense Journal.* This is done for convenience' sake, even though no cash is involved.

If the asset to be junked is fully depreciated, two entries are made under "General Ledger Items." In both entries, the amount to be entered is the original cost of the asset. One entry is made in the debit column, with the account shown as "Allowance for depreciation—[name of asset account]." The other entry is made in the credit column with the asset account shown.

If the asset is junked when it still has a book value, three entries are needed:

- The book value is entered in the debit column under "Miscellaneous Income and Expense Items," with the account shown as "Loss on abandonment of property."
- The cost of the asset is entered in the credit column under "General Ledger Items" with the asset account shown.
- The accumulated allowance for depreciation is entered in the

debit column under "General Ledger Items," with the account shown as "Allowance for depreciation—[name of asset account]."

Any loss on abandonment of property should be kept in a separate account from losses on sale of property. Under some circumstances, the two types of losses are treated differently for tax purposes.

RECORDING DISPOSAL OF PROPERTY ON THE DEPRECIATION SCHEDULE

Disposal of an asset must be recorded on the depreciation schedule as well as in the journals. The entries on the schedule remove the cost basis of the property from the "Cost" column, the depreciation allowed to the date of the disposal from the "Allowance for Depreciation" column, and any remaining depreciation from years' depreciation columns. Gain or loss on the disposal will neither affect nor appear on the depreciation schedule.

Referring to Exhibit 17, suppose that the delivery truck that was purchased in 1970 had been disposed of on July 1, 1974. At that time, depreciation of this truck accounted for $3,200 of the "Allowance for Depreciation" balance: $400 in 1970, $800 each year for the next three years, and $400 for six months of 1974. Therefore, the following entries, all deductions, will be made on the depreciation schedule (see "7-1-74" entry on Exhibit 17):

- $4,500 in the "Cost" column
- $3,200 in the "Allowance for Depreciation" column
- $400 in the "1974" column, to eliminate the last half year's depreciation
- $400 in the "1975" column
- $500 in the "Remaining Balance" column

These entries will be the same regardless of whether the truck was sold, traded in, or junked and regardless of whether or not it was disposed of at a profit. If the truck is traded in, the new truck will be entered on the depreciation schedule with the cost recorded as the book value of the old truck (in the above example $1,300) plus the cash paid.

All entries of disposals on the depreciation schedules should show the date of disposal and the year in which the property was purchased.

PART X
HERE THEY COME—TAXES!

27
Collecting and Recording Sales Taxes

A majority of the fifty states and many cities or other local jurisdictions have sales taxes. In some cases, both state and local taxes are assessed. It is usually the duty of the retailer to collect these taxes.

A number of factors complicate the collection and recording of sales taxes. Few if any states have one flat sales-tax rate for all sales. There may be more than one tax rate, depending on the type of item sold, and some items may be entirely exempt from the sales tax.

There are also exemptions based on the status of the purchaser. These might include sales to governmental agencies, certain public institutions, foreign diplomats, and persons who will resell goods. Often individual sales of very small amounts are tax-exempt.

The element of "breakage" also complicates the recording and reporting of sales-tax collections. Computing a sales tax exactly by applying the tax rate to the amount of the sale would often give fractions of cents. Because of this, most taxing jurisdictions specify sales-amount brackets to which certain amounts of taxes apply. Fractions of cents are usually rounded to the next higher cent in these tables, so that a little more than the tax rate is collected. Where the retailer is allowed to compute the amount he owes by applying the tax rate to his total taxable sales, a certain amount of breakage will accrue to the benefit of the retailer.

METHODS OF HANDLING SALES TAXES

The first requirement of the system you use for collecting, recording, and reporting sales taxes is that the system must meet the requirements of the taxing jurisdiction in which your business is located. Get in touch with the taxing authorities in your area for sales-tax regulations. If there is any doubt in your mind as to whether the system you want to use meets the requirements, describe it to the taxing authorities and ask them for suggestions.

Several different systems of recording sales-tax collections are described here. Which one is best suited to your needs will depend on the nature of your business and the sales-tax regulations in your area.

Method 1:   You can use this method of recording sales taxes if (1) all your sales are subject to sales tax and (2) a separate accounting for sales-tax collections is not required by law. When you ring up a sale on the cash register or prepare a sales check, compute the sales tax and record it as a part of the total sales. This means that the sales figures entered on the *Daily Summary* will include the sales tax.

After the month's transactions have been entered in the *Cash Receipts Journal*, compute the total sales tax for the month as follows:

1. Add the "Total Sales" column. This will give a preliminary total that includes the sales tax.
2. Divide this preliminary total by one plus the sales-tax rate to get the sales-only figure.
3. Multiply the sales-only figure by the sales-tax rate to get the sales tax.

You can check your computation by adding the sales tax to the sales-only figure. This should give the original column total.

For example, suppose the "Total Sales" column adds up to $106,000.00. With a sales-tax rate of 6 percent, the sales tax is computed as follows:

Sales only = $106,000 ÷ 1.06 = $100,000
Sales tax = $100,000 × .06 = $6,000
Check: $100,000 + $6,000 = $106,000

To enter the sales tax in the *Sales and Cash Receipts Journal,* write "Sales tax" in the description column and enter the sales-tax amount (1) in the "Total Sales" column, in parentheses or in red to show a deduction, and (2) in the credit column under "General Ledger Items." The "General Ledger" item will be posted to a liability account headed "Sales tax payable."

Method 2:   If almost all of your sales are subject to sales tax but an occasional tax-exempt sale occurs, method 1 can still be used with a little modification. A record is kept of all tax-exempt sales, both charge and cash. At the end of the month, these sales are totaled and subtracted from the total of the "Total Sales" column in the *Cash Receipts Journal.* The resulting figure will include only taxable sales and sales tax and is used instead of the column total in computing the amount of the sales tax.

Method 3:   If a substantial number of your sales are subject to sales tax but also a substantial number are not, you may have to record taxable sales and sales-tax collections separately. If you use sales checks, this is simply a matter of totaling tax-exempt sales, taxable sales, and sales-tax collections separately. If you use a cash register, you can have it equipped with taxable-sales and sales-tax keys. Each taxable item is rung up on the taxable-sales key. If a sale includes more than one taxable item, a subtotal of all these items is obtained and the tax computed for this subtotal. The sales tax is then rung up on the sales-tax key.

If you use this method, the *Daily Summary of Sales and Cash Receipts* should be revised to provide a separate record of taxable sales and sales tax. Separate columns should also be provided in the *Sales and Cash Receipts Journal* for total taxable sales and total sales tax.

The "Taxable Sales" column in the journal will be a memo column only to accumulate the amount to show on your sales-tax report. It is not used in preparing your monthly statements nor posted to the *General Ledger*. The "Sales Tax" column will be posted to the *General Ledger* account "Sales Tax Payable."

Method 4: If only a small percentage of your sales are subject to sales tax, you may find it satisfactory just to keep a list of the individual taxable sales (cash and charge) and the taxes on them. The taxes shown on this list can be totaled at the end of the month and entered in the *Sales and Cash Receipts Journal* as in method 1.

Other Methods: Several other methods or variations of the above methods could be used. For example, if your business is departmentalized, one department may sell almost entirely non-taxable items and another almost entirely taxable items. It may be possible to arrange the departments so that one or more of them sells entirely nontaxable items. No record of sales taxes would then have to be kept in these departments.

RECORDING PAYMENT OF SALES TAXES

When and how you pay sales taxes will depend on the regulations of the taxing authority in your area. Be sure that you understand what is required of you.

When you make the payment, it will be entered in the *Cash Disbursements Journal.* The account is shown as "Sales tax," and the amount is entered in the "Amount of Check" column and in the debit column under "General Ledger Items." The debit entry will later be posted to the "Sales Tax Payable" account in the *General Ledger.*

28
Payroll Records and Payroll Taxes

If you have any employees at all, you have certain obligations to the federal government for payment of payroll taxes and withholding of income taxes in connection with the salaries of your employees. You will probably have similar obligations for payroll and/or withholding taxes to the state and perhaps to the local jurisdiction; it depends on where your business is located. Contact city and state authorities for information about payroll and withholding taxes under their jurisdictions.

Federal regulations do not prescribe the form in which your payroll records must be kept, but the records should include the following information and documents:

1. the name, address, and Social Security number of each employee
2. the amount and date of each wage payment and the period covered by the payment
3. the amount of wages subject to withholding included in each payment
4. the amount of withholding tax collected and the date it was collected

5. if applicable, the reason that the taxable amount is less than the total payment
6. your employer identification number
7. duplicate copies of returns filed
8. dates and amounts of deposits made with government depositories
9. the periods for which your employees are paid by you while they are absent because of sickness or personal injury, and, for accident or health plans, information about the amount of each payment
10. your employees' withholding allowance certificates (Form W-4)
11. any agreement between you and an employee for withholding of additional amount of tax

You will also have to keep these documents and records:

1. copies of statements furnished by employees relating to nonresident alien status, residence in Puerto Rico or the Virgin Islands, or residence or physical presence in a foreign country
2. the value and date of any noncash compensation paid to a retail commission salesperson from which no tax was withheld
3. the dates in each calendar quarter on which an employee performed services not in the course of your trade or business, and the amount you paid for these services
4. copies of employees' statements of tips they received in the course of their employment, unless this information is reported on another item in this list
5. employees' requests to have their withholding tax computed on the basis of their cumulative wages or under the part-year employment method
6. The W-5 Forms (Earned Income Credit Advance Payment Certificate) of your employees who are eligible for the earned income credit and who wish to receive their payment

in advance rather than when they file their income-tax returns

Regarding Social Security (FICA) taxes, you must maintain these additional records:

1. the amount of wages that are subject to FICA tax
2. the amount and date of FICA employee tax collected for each payment and the date collected
3. if applicable, the reason that the total wage payment and the taxable amount are not equal

Under the Federal Unemployment Tax Act, you must maintain these records:

1. the total amount you paid your employees during the calendar year
2. the amount of the wages subject to the unemployment tax, and if applicable, why this amount differs from the total compensation
3. the amount you paid into the state unemployment fund, showing the payments deducted or to be deducted, and the payments not deducted or to be deducted from your employees' wages

PAYROLL RECORDS

Usually an *earnings card* is set up for each employee. Every wage payment to the employee is recorded on this card: all the information needed for meeting federal, state, and city requirements relating to payroll and withholding taxes, and all other amounts deducted from the employee's wages.

A number of payroll-records systems are available commercially. If you have only one or two employees, however, it should not be necessary to have a special payroll system. Paychecks can be entered directly in your *Cash Disbursements Journal* as described in Part III and on an earnings card for each employee. Earnings cards are available from most stationers who handle office supplies.

If you do not want to enter the individual employees' wages in the *Cash Disbursements Journal,* they can be entered on the earnings cards only. The gross salaries, each type of deduction, and net salaries can then be totaled, and the totals entered in the journal.

PAYROLL TAXES

There are three types of federal payroll taxes: (1) income taxes withheld, (2) Social Security taxes, and (3) federal unemployment taxes.

The rates as well as the bases for each of these taxes change from time to time as new legislation is passed. Publication 15 (Circular E), *Employer's Tax Guide,* published by the IRS, gives detailed instructions about these obligations.

As an employer, you are in effect an agent for the government in collecting income and Social Security taxes. As these taxes accumulate, you must deposit them in a bank that is authorized to collect them, either a Federal Reserve bank or an authorized financial institution.

Recording Payroll Taxes: Your bookkeeping can be simplified to some extent if at the end of each month you draw the required check to the depository and enter it for that month in the *Cash Disbursements Journal.* The entries are as follows:

Amount entered	Column
total amount of check	"Amount of Check"
amount representing income taxes withheld	"Payroll Deductions— Income tax" [as a deduction]
amount representing Social Security tax deducted from employees' wages	"Payroll Deductions— Social Security" [as a deduction]
amount representing your share of the Social Security tax	"Miscellaneous Income and Expense Items" [debit]

The total of the last three items should equal the amount of the check. If this is done every month, the deductions in the two "Payroll Deductions" columns will exactly offset all other entries in these columns. The columns will total zero and so will not have to be posted to the *General Ledger*.

State income taxes withheld are handled in much the same way, except that payments will probably be required only at the end of the quarter, since unemployment taxes are usually paid quarterly also.

Both federal and state unemployment taxes are an expense to you as the employer. They are entered in the *Cash Disbursements Journal*, with the description "Payroll taxes." The amounts of the payments should be entered in the "Amount of Check" column and also in the debit column under "Miscellaneous Income and Expense Items."

29
Income and
Self-Employment Taxes

The discussion of federal income taxes presented here does not go into technical instructions for preparing your tax returns. These instructions are best obtained from Publication 334, *Tax Guide for Small Business*, issued each year by the IRS.

Requirements for preparing and filing federal income-tax returns are more complicated for a business than for an individual. In deciding whether to prepare your own tax returns or hire someone to do it, you should consider the complexity of your business and whether you or one of your employees has the necessary skills. Usually a more accurate return can be prepared by someone who is thoroughly familiar with federal income-tax regulations. Many attorneys specialize in income-tax work, and nearly all practicing certified public accountants and public accountants prepare many tax returns each year.

TYPES OF FEDERAL INCOME-TAX RETURNS

The type of federal income-tax return you file will generally be governed by the form of your business organization. If your business is operated as an *individual proprietorship* (that is, if you are the sole owner and the business is not incorporated) you will report your business operations on Schedule C, to be attached to the Form 1040 you file as an individual.

If your business is a *partnership*, the business must file a Form 1065. No federal income tax has to be paid by the partnership as such, but the individual partners will report their shares of the profit or loss of the partnership on the Form 1040 which they file as individuals.

If your business is a *corporation*, the corporation must file a Form 1120 or 1120A. *S corporations* use Form 1120S. Any salaries or dividends paid by the corporation to you must be reported on the Form 1040 that you file as an individual.

Corporation tax returns are due on the fifteenth day of the third month following the close of the taxable year; individual and partnership returns, a month later.

SELF-EMPLOYMENT TAXES

If you are the owner of an individual proprietorship or if you are a partner in a partnership, the amounts you withdraw from the business are not reportable for the federal payroll taxes discussed in the preceding chapter of this book. However, unless you had wages from another source subject to the maximum amount reportable for Social Security taxes, you will have to pay, in place of Social Security taxes, a *self-employment tax* based on your income from the business. Although the self-employment tax is not an income tax, the computation is done on Schedule SE (Form 1040) and filed with your individual federal income-tax return.

DECLARATION OF ESTIMATED TAXES

If you are self-employed, you may be required to file a declaration of estimated tax, even though a wage earner with the same income would not have to do so. This is because income taxes are not withheld from your self-employment income as they are in the case of a wage earner. Current law and regulations require that you file a declaration and make quarterly payments on the estimated tax if your estimated income tax and self-employment tax will exceed your total withholding and credits by $500 or more.

STATE INCOME TAXES

Most states and some local jurisdictions have an income tax applicable to businesses. In some cases, the tax returns are very much like those used for federal taxes. In other areas, an entirely different approach is used. Many states also require information returns.

Contact the local tax authorities in your area and find out what requirements apply to your business. If these requirements differ from those for federal income-tax returns, make sure that your recordkeeping system will give you the necessary information.

RECORDING INCOME TAXES

If your business is an individual proprietorship or a partnership, you ordinarily will not record these taxes on your business books. However, if the business pays taxes as a corporation, the taxes should be entered as an expense of the business. They should be recorded each month so that your monthly statements of profit and loss will not be misleading.

The exact amount of the tax, of course, cannot be computed until the end of the year, so the monthly tax entries will have to be estimated. This can be done as follows:

1. Estimate your total profit for the year and the tax on this profit.
2. Divide the estimated tax by the estimated profit.
3. Multiply the month's profit by the answer obtained in step 2.

In estimating the federal income tax for the year, be sure to take into account any losses carried over from previous years. These could reduce or eliminate entirely the tax being estimated. Also, your business might show a loss for one or more months during the year. If that happens, no income tax is entered for those months. Instead, a deduction may have to be entered to reduce the income taxes entered for previous months to the point where the year-to-date tax is the correct percentage of the year-to-date profit. State income taxes are handled in the same manner.

The sum of the estimated state and federal income taxes for the month (if both are applicable) is entered on line 25 of the monthly Profit-and-Loss Statement (Exhibit 7). It is also entered in the *Cash Disbursements Journal*—in the debit column under "Miscellaneous Income and Expense Items," described as "Income taxes," and in the credit column under "General Ledger Items," described as "Income tax payable." If the month's operations resulted in a loss instead of a profit and the income tax set up in earlier months had to be reduced, the entry under "Miscellaneous Income and Expense Items" is in the credit column and the one under "General Ledger Items" in the debit column.

For Further Information

If you are interested in further study of basic double-entry book-keeping, your local library will be able to provide you with accounting textbooks. There are many good ones.

The IRS publications already mentioned in Parts IX and X of the text are essential. They are

Tax Information on Depreciation—Publication 534
Tax Guide for Small Business—Publication 334
Employer's Tax Guide—Publication 15 (Circular E)
Sales and Other Dispositions of Assets—Publication 544

These publications are available free from local offices of the Internal Revenue Service or from the U.S. Treasury Department, Internal Revenue Service, Washington, D.C. 20224.

Some private companies and trade associations have published recordkeeping systems for specific types of business. For a list of some of these systems, see "Recordkeeping System: Small Store and Service Trade" *(Small Business Bibliography No. 15)*. This list is available for a small processing fee. Order forms 115A and 115B are available free from the U.S. Small Business Administration, Box 15434, Fort Worth, Texas 76119.